The incredible life
and adventures
of Steve and Terri Irwin

The Crocodile Hunter™

STEVE & TERRI IRWIN

NAL
BOOKS

NEW AMERICAN LIBRARY

New American Library
Published by New American Library, a division of
Penguin Group (USA) Inc., 375 Hudson Street,
New York, New York 10014, USA
Penguin Group (Canada), 10 Alcorn Avenue, Toronto,
Ontario M4V 3B2, Canada (a division of Pearson Penguin Canada Inc.)
Penguin Books Ltd., 80 Strand, London WC2R 0RL, England
Penguin Ireland, 25 St. Stephen's Green, Dublin 2,
Ireland (a division of Penguin Books Ltd.)
Penguin Group (Australia), 250 Camberwell Road, Camberwell, Victoria 3124,
Australia (a division of Pearson Australia Group Pty. Ltd.)
Penguin Books India Pvt. Ltd., 11 Community Centre, Panchsheel Park,
New Delhi - 110 017, India
Penguin Group (NZ), cnr Airborne and Rosedale Roads, Albany,
Auckland 1310, New Zealand (a division of Pearson New Zealand Ltd.)
Penguin Books (South Africa) (Pty.) Ltd., 24 Sturdee Avenue,
Rosebank, Johannesburg 2196, South Africa

Penguin Books Ltd., Registered Offices:
80 Strand, London WC2R 0RL, England

Published by New American Library, a division of Penguin Group (USA) Inc. Previously published in a Dutton edition. Originally published in New Zealand by Penguin Group (NZ).

First New American Library Printing, November 2002
10 9 8 7 6 5

 REGISTERED TRADEMARK—MARCA REGISTRADA

New American Library Trade Paperback ISBN: 0-451-20673-8

The Library of Congress has catalogued the hardcover edition of this title as follows:

Irwin, Steve.
   The crocodile hunter : the incredible life and adventures of Steve and Terri Irwin / Steve and Terri Irwin.
   p.cm
ISBN 0-525-94635-7 (alk. paper)
1. Irwin, Steve. 2. Irwin, Terri. 3. Herpetologists—Australia—Biography. 4. Dangerous animals. I. Irwin, Terri. II. Title.
QL31.I78 A3 2001
597.9'092—dc21   2001040124
[B]

Designed by Anthony Ramondo

Printed in the United States of America

I'm dedicating this book, and my life, to my mum. I loved my mum more than anything in the world. She nurtured, protected, and loved me all my life. Lyn Irwin was a true "Australian Pioneer Woman," dedicating her entire life to the rehabilitation and conservation of both the wildlife and her family. Every single day she worked and toiled to save injured and orphaned joeys while maintaining a happy healthy Irwin clan.

Oh gosh! I miss you, Mum. I miss you every minute of every day, and the pain of losing you tears my heart out. But I'll stay strong, I promise you I'll stay strong—for it was you who taught me to be a "Wildlife Warrior."

You worked with me for thirty-eight years to help me become the man I am today. You suckled me, changed my nappy, packed me off to school, blessed me with a career that is my whole life, cried with me when my pet snake died, belted me with your shoe when I was really naughty, fought for me, protected me, pushed me forward when the going got tough, and raised me to fight for the preservation of wildlife until the day I die.

I've adopted your strength, your passion and enthusiasm, your dedication and commitment, and will honor your presence by continuing to push forward as hard and fast as I possibly can, to ensure the survival of our precious wildlife, the wilderness, and in essence, the human race. For without fresh water, trees, animals, and ecosystems, the world we now know would not support human life; it would be an ugly, awful place. The spirit of Lynette Leslie Irwin, Lyn Irwin, my mum, lives forever. Every time you see a sick, injured, orphaned animal, you'll see Lyn. I love you, I miss you, I long to be reunited with you.

—Steve

CONTENTS

Introduction

The Dream Begins

The Irwin crocodile story begins with my parents, Bob and Lyn Irwin. Keen naturalists and herpetologists, they had three children: Joy, myself, and Mandy. I was to grow up following in my father's footsteps. In November 1970, when Bob, Lyn, and I were on a field trip to catch snakes in southeast Queensland, my parents purchased the property that was to become Australia Zoo.

My dad, Robert Eric Irwin, was born and raised in the state of Victoria in the Dandenong Ranges by his mum, my grandma, during the Depression. His dad and his grandfather (Ronald and George Joseph Irwin) both died while fighting in Southeast Asia against the Japanese during World War II.

It's a very Australian tradition to shorten people's names or adopt a nickname, so my dad was always affectionately known as Bob. He grew up during very, very rough times. His mum, Marjorie Irwin, had lost her husband and father-in-law to the war, and had virtually no money while trying to raise her two sons. She was made of the right stuff and struggled through those tough times, raising Bob

Mum and Dad, young lovers.

up to be a fine young man, an exceptional plumber, and a lover of the Australian bush and its reptiles.

My mum, Lynette Leslie Irwin, was raised by my nanna and pa, Vesta and Frank Hakainsson, in the town of Boronia near where Bob lived. Pa also served during World War II, and as luck would have it, he was injured and returned home to his family. Lyn, as she was affectionately known, grew up to become a maternity nurse with a passion for sick and orphaned wildlife.

Bob and Lyn were friends as kids, and their friendship developed into love as teenagers—they were destined to spend their lives together. They married when Dad was twenty and Mum was eighteen years old, and they started a family straightaway. Dad continued as a very successful plumber and their business flourished. The whole time, Dad's passion for reptiles was accelerating at an alarming rate. He was nurturing an ever-increasing collection of snakes in our family home at Essendon, south of Melbourne, the capital of Victoria.

On my sixth birthday I was given a gift from my dad and mum that was to be the start of our animal collection fauna park. I was totally excited to receive a twelve-foot scrub python, although the difference in our sizes meant that I couldn't in fact play with it, or I might have become its next meal! My snake's name was Fred and I loved him dearly, despite the drawbacks attached, with him seeing me as a potential food source.

Our menagerie grew over the next two years. Dad and I were passionate about catching snakes and lizards. I remember a classic encounter with a brown snake that was to become an important member of our family. Dad and a seven-year-old Steve were in the bush in northern Victoria searching for snakes and as we traveled along a granite boulder-encrusted creek, I pretended I was in the army. Stalking a preoccupied Dad was always great: he would be the enemy and I'd grab a well-shaped stick or branch, which would be my submachine gun or .303. This particular afternoon I'd scampered up some boulders and set up in an ambush position. As I took aim with my "gun" I noticed a nearly seven-foot brown snake tongue-flicking my foot. Wearing only plastic sandals, the flesh of my feet was totally exposed. After a few moments of tongue-flicking, which is the snake's method of smelling, the huge brown decided I wasn't edible, nor was I an immediate threat. It started to retreat down a rabbit burrow where it would certainly have disappeared, but without any hesitation, I pinned it with my foot about mid-body so it couldn't escape. It hissed in anger.

"Dad! Dad! *Dad!* I've got one, I've got one, Dad!" I yelled out.

"Where are you?"

"Dad! Dad! Quick! I've got a brown snake!" I shouted.

Several minutes lapsed and then I could see Dad running for all he was worth up the boulders. I could feel the pride and adrenaline building. Not even watching the snake, I shouted down to him.

"I've got a big brown snake!"

"Where?" he replied, struggling for breath.

"I've got a big one right here."

Mum and Dad with my sixth birthday present: Fred, a scrub python. The difference in our sizes, however, meant that I couldn't in fact play with it!

He couldn't see my lower body and was now within feet of me.

"Where?" he asked again as he came over the last boulder to my level.

"Here," I pointed.

Thump! The power of his forearm against my shoulder knocked me airborne. I crashed into the unforgiving rock, and my arm went dead from the impact of Dad hitting me. My knees were skinned.

"You bloody idiot!" he screamed at me.

The pain from my injuries disappeared as the pain from his anger crushed me like a bug.

"But Dad," I whimpered.

My heart was broken, my pride had turned into an overwhelming sense of confusion and embarrassment. Bursting into an uncontrollable state of crying, I ran off down the rocks. I ran and ran, bawling my eyes out. Finally, I had to stop running as I was crying so hard I couldn't get my breath. I was sobbing so much my breathing was impaired and I didn't know what to do.

I'll run away, I thought. That's it, I'll run away. If I run away, that'll show him. I'll just keep heading up this creek and no one will ever find me.

Pretty soon, the minutes seemed like hours and I'd regained my breath and stopped crying. I'm going to find a cave and live in it forever, I decided.

Looking around, I spotted a huge crack in the rocks and headed toward it, hoping it might lead me to my cave. As I stuck my head inside the cave, I sensed movement. Sure enough, I spotted some beady little eyes staring back at me. Wow! Skinks. Cunninghams skinks. The crack I was now well and truly entrenched in housed several of these beautiful little lizards. My despair waned as enthusiasm and fascination took control of my thoughts once more.

After what seemed to be hours, but was probably only half an hour of coaxing the lizards with strands of grass, I couldn't dislodge them. They hadn't budged an inch. The sound of Dad's car horn echoed through the boulders. It was getting dark.

"Goodbye, little lizards," I sighed, then took off as fast as my legs could carry me toward the car.

Reaching the car, I jumped in quickly. I was too scared to say anything. I knew Dad's silence meant he was angry with me. It wasn't until my late teens that I realized what had happened that day.

Brown snakes are the second most venomous snake in the world. They cause more fatal snakebites in Australia than any other snake. They are considered aggressive and lethal if cornered or molested. Pinning that brown snake in the middle of the body should have cost me a bite, and possibly my life. When Dad looked down, the angry brown snake had been about to bite my foot.

I'd been warned time and time again prior to this incident to never touch a venomous snake. Even at seven years of age I could identify any snake and should have known better. Dad probably saved my life by knocking me over—thank God for his reflexes. This particular snake was one of the first venomous snakes in our menagerie.

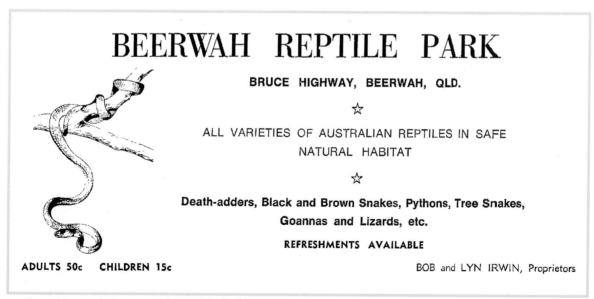

BEERWAH REPTILE PARK

BRUCE HIGHWAY, BEERWAH, QLD.

☆

ALL VARIETIES OF AUSTRALIAN REPTILES IN SAFE
NATURAL HABITAT

☆

**Death-adders, Black and Brown Snakes, Pythons, Tree Snakes,
Goannas and Lizards, etc.**

REFRESHMENTS AVAILABLE

ADULTS 50c   CHILDREN 15c   BOB and LYN IRWIN, Proprietors

One of the early brochures for the Park. After a year of hard work my parents opened what has now become Australia Zoo, which Terri and I operate today.

Dad with a goanna. My parents are both keen naturalists with a particular passion for reptiles and amphibians.

Within a few years our collection of reptiles and other animals had grown to the stage where bedrooms weren't big enough to house everything. So Dad and Mum made the biggest decision of their lives—to move to the Sunshine Coast and start up a wildlife sanctuary. They chose a beautiful four-acre paddock covered in lush tropical flora in 1970.

It took Dad a solid three years of hard yakka (labor) to establish the foundations of what is now the most popular private zoological facility and park in Australia. I helped him build everything, though I was probably more of a hindrance than a help. But I kept Dad amused. Of course, Dad knew he needed to be enthusiastic about my helping him, as it's during these younger years that a young fella develops work ethics and skills. I worked hard and was rewarded with field trips.

In those early days Dad and I shared the most marvelous adventures. We'd travel the Aussie outback for weeks at a time, catching crocs, snakes, and lizards for the park. I'd help Mum raise orphan joey kangaroos and wallabies and spend endless nights rehabilitating injured birds and other animals. Our park grew and flourished from the day the gates were opened in 1973, but it never ceases to impress me how our menagerie grew into a zoo. Dad's dream came true; he'd always wanted his own reptile park in Queensland and it was his hard work and careful planning that made it a reality. The initial name of the park was the Beerwah Reptile Park and our first postcard is a classic reminder of those "good old days." Dad and Mum started with a piece of dirt and within six months we got the park open.

"We'll have to learn as we go," was Dad's motto. That's exactly what we did and continue to do.

Mum feeding her orphaned joey swamp wallaby.

Chapter I

The Early Years

The early years of the Beerwah Reptile Park were total wildlife experiences, so many that my memory will be recalling them till the day I die. Too many phenomenal wildlife experiences to ever remember and record in the rest of my life—but I'll give it a go anyway.

I remember my dad being recognized as the greatest herpetologist (one who studies reptiles) in Australia and revered throughout the world as a legend for catching highly venomous snakes, with nothing more than his bare hands and sharp reflexes. I used to watch in awe, in an adrenaline-filled stare, as Dad captured fierce snakes—taipans, browns, tigers, and death adders—the most venomous snakes in the world—in wilderness, rural, and urban areas all over Australia.

My dad, my hero.

His passion, enthusiasm, skill, and greatness with venomous snakes are an innate, natural, God-given ability, which unbeknownst to me, was also in my veins, heart, and soul.

Curley the Curlew looking after an orphaned joey grey kangaroo.

By staring at and mimicking my dad, my own instinctive ability with snakes and virtually all wildlife began to develop. Little did I know that my dad was my mentor, and all those early years when I was a kid, he and Mum were gearing me up to become a wildlife guru like them.

What a childhood! My mum was a pioneer in Australian history. She was the Mother Teresa of wildlife rehabilitation. Way back in the late sixties and early seventies, very little to nothing was known about caring for or raising orphaned kangaroos, wallabies, koalas, wombats, platypuses, snakes, and lizards. This was unknown territory that my mum pioneered with brilliance and innovation. She developed pouches for kangaroo babies, known as joeys. She developed formulas and nursing techniques for orphaned koalas, and raised Sugar Gliders when scientists were still endeavoring to work out what they were. My mum *was* Mother Nature. Crikey, I love my mum and I am so sorry I can't

write every single detail and element of my love for her and the greatness of her work. To this day, I miss her so much, the pain is so strong, I can barely keep pen on paper. I'll swallow, I'll push back the tears, and continue.

Our house was a giant maternity ward fair smack-dab in the middle of the Beerwah

An orphaned koala hugging its teddy bear for security.

Reptile Park. It was nothing for us kids to be sharing our house with orphaned joey red and grey kangaroos who'd stayed in their dead mothers' pouches after they'd been killed on the road. Luckily enough we always stopped to check on the road-killed mothers, and other good Samaritans were constantly bringing joeys they'd found in to us. There'd be three orphaned Sugar Gliders and a couple of ringtail or brushtail possums that would need feeding and a play at night, koala joeys that Mum was raising because dogs had killed their mummas, six baby birds, untold amounts of other orphans, babies, and injured Australian animals constantly sharing our house. What a wild menagerie and an exceptional household to be raised in. Imagine the skills and hands-on experience I was getting as a child—soaking up all this pioneering, virtually unteachable, incredibly important information that could only be learned by living in my mum's rehabilitation world—a wildlife orphanage.

Am I the luckiest bloke in the entire world? Yes! I totally believe I am and I owe it all to my dad and mum and, of course, fate. My destiny—my path in this life, in this world—was chosen for me. All I had to do was walk the path and live my life. I became the man I was always meant to be. Thanks Dad and thank you, Mum, I love you dearly.

From 1970 onward, our entire lives were dedicated to one all-important common goal: the Beerwah Reptile

Dad at the original Beerwah Reptile Park entrance.

A juvenile freshwater crocodile. What a little beauty!

Park and wildlife conservation. Each and every day we strove for excellence and innovation in educating people about our precious Australian wildlife.

I've got the wildest childhood memories. My Dad, Bob Irwin, is recognized as a legendary herpetologist, pioneering venomous snake and crocodile capture techniques. Before I was ten, Dad was spending more and more time teaching me how to jump and restrain crocodiles, and deal with the world's deadliest snakes without causing them stress and at the same time minimizing the chances of being bitten.

I remember my very first croc capture when I was nine years old. Dad had been asked by the Queensland National Parks and Wildlife Service and a local farmer to catch and relocate a small colony of freshwater crocs at the Leichhardt River System in the Gulf of Carpentaria, North Queensland.

There are two species of crocodile in Australia: the large, notorious, sometimes man-eating saltwater crocodile, and the less aggressive freshwater crocodile. Saltwater crocodiles always command respect as they are the "Kings of the North," and can grow to lengths in excess of twenty feet. The freshwater crocodile rarely grows more than ten feet. Commonly known as "freshies," they are considered harmless to humans if left alone. However, they are very powerful, compact crocs with rows of needle-sharp teeth, and if molested can cause nasty injuries.

The colony of freshies we were asked to capture and remove were about to lose their isolated waterhole; it was to be drained out and filled in. Our method of capture was one I still use to this day—spotlighting at night out of a small aluminium dinghy then jumping on the crocs.

Dad with a small "freshie" he caught, for relocation to the Park.

Over a couple of nights while moving the colony of freshwater crocs, I'd worked at carefully and quietly idling the boat in the direction of Dad's spotlight and the crocodile's eyeshine. As we got closer and closer, Dad would poise himself at the front of the boat and put his spotlight down as I'd bring mine up. Closer, closer, I'd idle the boat right at the red glowing eyeshine. Just as I'd lose sight of the eyeshine under the front of the boat, Dad would spear himself right on top of the crocodile. Grabbing it around the neck, he'd use his legs and body to restrain the frantic croc. Once it had tired and Dad was in control he'd call to me, "It's comin' in." He'd flip the croc straight into the boat, at which point I'd jump on it with all my weight and hang on. Restraining it on the floor of the boat was wild; I'd get thrashed around all over the paddock but I wouldn't let go. I'd hang on regardless of the consequences

Dad, Mum, and me removing skin from a 20-foot reticulated python.

because I knew that in a very short time Dad would be back in the boat to help.

Dad would secure blindfolds on the crocs to settle them down and to minimize their stress, then he'd pop them into a bag. We were quite a team—the "bring 'em back alive" team.

And so on the day I first captured a croc myself, Dad was securing a croc in a bag while I scanned the waterhole for more eyeshine.

"There's one," I whispered.

"Looks like a little beauty!" Dad replied.

"About a three-footer, I reckon," I whispered, now with some experience in my voice.

"You get up the front of the boat and hold the eyeshine with the spotty!" Dad commanded.

Without knowing what was about to happen, I did just that. Dad pointed the boat straight at the croc and idled up closer and closer. Frozen in position, and with eyes as big as dinner plates, I focused on the eyeshine as it grew brighter and brighter. We were within twenty feet of the croc when I twigged: I'm in the wrong position—I should be driving!

Next thing I knew Dad's spotty was glowing over my right shoulder, right onto the croc. "Righto, son, I've got him, down spotlight."

Without the slightest sound I flicked my spotty off and placed it down. "Get up there, boy." Without a moment's thought I positioned myself in the jumping position.

Dad and me checking a net for freshwater crocodiles in the Gulf of Carpentaria.

"Wait . . . wait for it . . . wait."

I couldn't wait, I could feel myself readying to jump.

"Wait, son, wait."

I could see the long narrow jaws and the white of the croc's teeth in the powerful beam of the torch.

"Now!" he shouted.

I'm pretty sure I was airborne even before the command.

My fingers clamped around the croc's thick neck and my chin slammed into its bony head as my chest landed on its back and my legs wrapped around the base of the tail. With eyes wide open I was being thrashed around in the muddy water. I saw pulses of light as I was rolled over and over. There was no way I was letting go and I hung on for grim death.

"I've gotcha, I've gotcha," I bubbled. Just as the reality of being an air-breathing human started to be felt, I sensed the strength and warmth of my Dad's arm feeling for my body. *Whoosh!* Dad's forearm locked around my side and next thing both croc and I were slammed into the floor of the boat. He pinned both croc and me to the floor with his big calloused hands.

"Are ya all right?"

"Yeah, I got him, Dad."

As Dad placed his spotty on the seat and started securing a blindfold and bag, he kept the weight of one hand on my back, keeping both croc and me pinned to the floor. He looked down at us and then stopped what he was doing. As I looked up to see what was wrong, I saw his face in the beam. He was shaking his head in disbelief with a grin from ear to ear. I could feel his pride in me although the capture had certainly made him a little nervous. While I was under the water wrestling the croc he could neither see nor feel me. But he never intimated any concern at all. He's one tough old bastard, my dad.

That was the start of my croc-jumping career. By the age of twelve I'd become quite skilled at spearing myself out of the front of a boat, and took this responsibility very seriously.

Following in my father's footsteps wasn't all glory. One weekend while playing schoolboy cricket, I was called up to bat at second drop. I padded up, keen to score a century. Second ball and I was out for a duck. Disappointed and bored with the game, I started searching the nearby creek hoping to find some lizards to chase. Turning over an old sheet of corrugated iron, I spotted a beautiful little gecko. It spotted me and made a run for it. As I pounced and missed the gecko, I felt something soft under my elbow, and then heard a hiss. The hackles on the back of my neck shot up as a huge red-bellied black snake flattened out into the strike position. I had unknowingly landed with all my weight right on top of a now very angry snake. Realizing that my face was well within strike range, I gently lifted my elbow, stopped breathing and braced for a bite to the head. The snake hissed vehemently but allowed me to pull back out of range. Wow! Am I lucky, I thought.

I was now at a safe distance from the snake. I'll catch it, I thought, I bet Dad would love a big red-bellied black. Without thinking twice, I went straight at the snake. It struck and

The red-bellied black snake is, in fact, very venomous and a bite could be fatal.

recoiled, ready to strike again. Briefly I pondered how I was going to catch this snake without getting bitten. I went at it again. It struck and glanced off my boot then recoiled back into the strike position. As I backed off, intimidated by the near-miss, the snake decided to make a dash for the long grass. As it slithered off toward the knee-high kikuyu grass, I thrust my hand through the blades of the grass and grabbed its tail. *Whoosh!* It launched a strike past my nose.

I regained my balance and began moving around the snake in circles, hanging onto its tail. I was careful to keep its body on the ground and allow its front half to get into the grass, just as I'd seen Dad do a million times. Now what, I thought, I've got no bag.

"Stumpy! Hey, Stumpy!" I screamed. My mate Stumpy, who was also waiting for our game, came charging up in response to my screams.

"Oh, my God!" he called in disbelief at the sight of me with this huge black snake.

"Get something to put it in!" I screamed.

Within a minute he returned with the bus driver's eskimo cooler.

"Good one, Stumpy. Take off the lid and empty out the food."

Without effort he flipped off the lid and upended the full esky. Drinks and sandwiches piled out on the ground.

"Now what?"

"Put the esky near my legs."

As he threw the esky at my feet, the snake pulled out of the grass and pivoted from its tail, which was in my hand, straight at the esky. It bit the esky then struck at me. I swung out of its way with another narrow miss.

"Give me the lid," I told Stumpy.

He threw the lid at me, shouting, "Let it go or it'll kill you!"

As the snake struck at me again, I stepped backward and it landed over the esky. I grabbed the lid and dropped the snake before it climbed off the esky. Then I slammed the lid down.

"Gotcha!"

During the next couple of hours I managed to locate and capture another six good-sized red-bellied blacks. The biggest problem was getting each one into the esky without the others flying out. A couple of times a snake would come out as I was putting one in. Toward the end of the day I was getting really good at it and had most of both cricket teams around me "ooohing" and "aaahing," scared but enthralled.

"Watch out, Steve."

"Look out, Steve."

"There's one getting out, Steve."

This was heaps more fun than playing cricket but pretty soon it was time to go home. Some of the boys dobbed me in to the bus driver.

"He's got snakes in your esky," they told him.

"Young Irwin, what have you got in my esky?"

"Well, sir, I've um, um, er . . ."

"Have you got snakes in my esky?"

"Yes, sir, but you can see how secure the lid is. They won't get out, I promise!"

"You're not taking bloody snakes on this bus! It's dangerous, get them out!" he shouted, fear in his voice.

But my mates pleaded with the bus driver, "Let him take the snakes, they're harmless."

(The red-bellied black snake is, in fact, very venomous and a bite could be fatal.) I said defensively, "Yes, sir, it's OK, they can't get out. I'll hold them till we get to my place."

"Bloody snakes," the bus driver muttered.

I'd never seen anyone drive a bus so quickly. He really planted his foot down, and we arrived back in no time. Excited, my cricket team and the bus driver escorted me into the Park where we met my dad.

"Your son's got these snakes in my esky, on my bus. I don't have to put up with this, he's endangered everyone's lives. I hate snakes. He's banned from my bus." The bus driver continued to carry on.

"Hang on, just hang on," Dad commanded. "*Have* you got snakes in there?" he questioned me.

"Yeah, Dad, I've got seven real nice red-bellies."

"Red-bellies!" he exploded. And before I could say any more, he'd sunk his boot right up my bum so hard I dropped the esky.

"But, Dad!"

"No buts! Get in the house, now!" he roared. "How dare you risk people's lives with your stupidity!"

Looking back I suppose it was pretty risky; I'd got caught up in the excitement and adrenaline of the capture and forgotten about the possible consequences of dealing with such a potentially dangerous animal. Funny thing, I wasn't too scared of dying from black snake envenomation, but I was shaking in my boots at the thought of losing Dad's pride in me, the bloke I respect and admire the most, the bloke responsible for the person I am today. It was another lesson well learned.

All my life I've followed in my dad's footsteps. I virtually worshipped the ground he walked on. He is my hero, my legend, my mentor, my best friend, and my father. All I've ever wanted to be is my dad, and every day in some way I mimic him, and grew up knowing that one day I was going to be just like him.

It's funny how my hardest yet most valuable lessons came from Dad when I was just a boy. At the time I couldn't quite understand that he was teaching me and saving my life—it felt more like I was just constantly in trouble. Throughout my boyhood, teenage and young adult life, my dad was very careful to nurture my instincts. He spotted natural instincts in me when I was very young and helped me to harness these innate powers.

As I've grown up, I guess I have indeed become my dad.

Growing up at the Park there was never a dull moment. I was surrounded by the best of friends, mates for life. My favorite and longtime companions were Curley, Egg Head, and Brolly, and playing armies with them was always great fun (and instrumental in my development of camouflage techniques as a boy). I always won the battles despite gunshot wounds and injuries sustained during hand-to-hand combat with dozens of enemy forces. My mates and I stuck together and we conquered all.

Curley was a bush-stoned curlew who thought she was an emu, Egg Head was an emu who thought he was a human, and Brolly was a brolga who thought he was the "ants pants," a real aristocrat who quickly tired of our imaginary games.

Two of my boyhood mates, Curley (above), the curlew who thought she was an emu, and (below) Brolly, a brolga.

So Curley, Egg Head, and I would be the good guys and quite often, because Brolly wouldn't come over to our side, he would be the enemy. Together we'd stalk, shoot, throw grenades, and fight hand-to-hand.

At least once a day things would get out of hand when Egg Head would try to kick the living daylights out of Brolly. Brolly would respond by stabbing us with his scissor-like beak.

Looking back at our antics, I'd hate to think how many times Curley and I got stomped into the ground by Egg Head, who often seemed to lose the plot, kicking and trampling all of us. Then throwing his little head into the air, he'd run, run, run for no apparent reason, stop, roll on his back, and kick his legs in the air. I guess it's an emu thing.

Playing marbles around an emu was always a challenge—Egg Head would sneak up and within seconds would have eaten up all my marbles. At first this was really annoying, but I quickly worked out that within a week he'd poo them all out. So I simply hosed the poo with water and regained my much-treasured marbles.

The fourth member of our gang was Egg Head, an emu who had an appetite for just about anything, including my marbles.

But other aspects of Egg Head's behavior were more worrying. One day I heard Dad shouting, "You stupid bird brain, get out of it!" Egg Head had snuck up and was eating Dad's nice shiny nails. That same day we had to catch and restrain our poor old emu when he stuck his whole head into a can of paint! An emu with a "Mission Brown"–painted head looks pretty funny, but it wasn't funny trying to hold him down and wipe it off, his eyes and beak sticking together as the paint dried. It was a traumatic experience but by the next day Egg Head had forgotten all about it and was keen to play armies again.

I grew up with a very strong sporting background—swimming, playing football, cricket, and

soccer and, later in life, surfing. Dad had been in the Australian badminton team and one day I decided to build a badminton court, Dad helping to put up the net and to mark out the boundaries with sand. Problem was, Brolly considered the sand pile as his. He would dance on his sand pile for hours, showing off to anyone or anything in the vicinity.

"Brolly, I'm taking some of your sand," I said.

Brolly spread his wings and jumped in the air, dancing and bugling in response. I guessed that this meant "no way" in brolga lingo but, determined, I gathered a bucketful of sand and started to mark out the boundaries. Brolly was very unhappy with this and stood in my path with his wings spread aggressively.

"Listen here, Brolly," I said, "if you're a good bird and let me build this court, we'll let you chase the shuttlecock and stab the net."

He seemed to understand exactly what I said, moved aside, and turned his back on me. "Thank you, you're such a clever bird," I remarked, but no sooner had I tipped out a handful of sand when, *whammo,* everything went black. The defiant Brolly had waited for his moment and then pecked me on the top of the head so hard it had knocked me down and out.

As I regained consciousness and my vision, the first thing I saw was Brolly dancing and flicking sand out of the bucket, obviously very proud of his win. I picked myself up off the ground and went running to Mum, blood streaming through my hair and down my face.

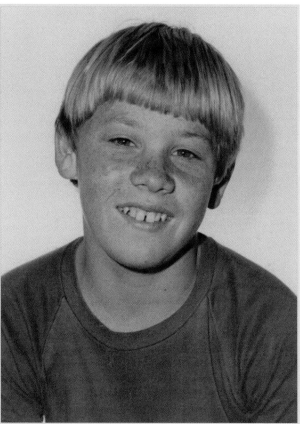

I was nine years old when I captured my first croc.

"Mum!" I cried. "Brolly stabbed me in the head and my brains will come out," I whimpered.

"Don't worry, son, you'll be all right, give me a look," she reassured me.

I was always injured and bleeding from somewhere. Once again, Mum cleaned me up and sent me on my way, as only a mother could.

"Now you respect Brolly's things. You wouldn't like it if he took your bike now, would you?" she explained.

To this day I still have some very memorable scar tissue on my head, but by the next day Brolly and I were mates again. I continue to respect an animal's space and belongings. Such trials and tribulations from those early years are now fond memories, forming lessons and experiences that in one way or another I utilize in everyday life, and which make me the bloke I am.

By 1980, the Beerwah Reptile Park had grown at an incredible rate and was upgraded to the Queensland Reptile and Fauna Park. We were a zoological facility like no other in the world. Our collection of beautiful Australian animals was made up of orphans that had been raised as my brothers and sisters, and reptiles that people despised were loved and welcomed into our family.

It was in the early eighties, when Mum and Dad were so desperately dedicated to rescuing, saving, and protecting all of Australia's wildlife, that a huge decision was about to be made.

Dad and I were out on a pineapple farmer's property trying to rescue a platypus that had lost his water hole, and the bulldozers were moving in. We were skirting the muddy banks, almost giving up hope of finding the poor little blighter. Something urged me to dive my hands into the mud to catch a yabby (a type of freshwater crayfish), and as I

grabbed the yabby, it hit me. I looked down into the greasy mud and saw movement. With the yabby still firmly clamped on my fingers, I reached into the mud and there she was—the most beautiful animal on earth, a very young female platypus. She was gorgeous.

"Dad, Dad, I got her!"

"You beauty!" he thundered back.

On our way to release her into a new water hole where she would be safe from bulldozers forever, Dad discussed his huge decision with me.

The platypus I rescued. Isn't she gorgeous?

Oh boy, here we go.

Dad and Mum were sick to death of people's hatred of the big saltwater crocodiles in far North Queensland. They couldn't stand it any longer. They decided now was the time to rescue crocs that were deemed dangerous and were to be eliminated. Their belief and aim was a massive move to boost conservation and education about crocodiles, to help crocodiles in need of new territories, and to educate people about the beauty of the greatest reptilian predator in the world.

It was in the early 1980s that Dad and I got deadly serious about capturing and relocating crocodiles that were deemed dangerous. He fired up his busted old backhoe and started digging water holes. We were building the Crocodile Environmental Park. To this day we're still building it—it will never be finished. The Queensland Reptile and Fauna Park was not about

catching a bunch of crocodiles and sticking them in cages for people to look at. No way—never. Not on your life.

We built croc territory for designated rogue or problem crocodiles that were destined to be shot or killed. We love crocs, always have and always will. Our passion for crocs is perpetual, and over these early years, Dad and myself rescued hundreds. All of the animals you see in our zoo needed our help, especially our crocs.

Dad on his backhoe constructing the "Crocodile Environmental Park."

Chapter II

The Acco Encounter

It was during the 1960s that stories first emerged of a huge black crocodile living in one of many river systems of North Queensland. Fishermen working the monster's remote tidal river system would return with yarns, reinforced by fear in their expressions, of narrow escapes and life-threatening battles with the marauding monster croc.

For over twenty years the legend of the big black croc sent shivers down the spines of North Queenslanders. He had sunk boats, torn up nets, driven fishermen from the river, and attacked and killed scrubber bulls, then dragged the carcasses hundreds of feet across mudflats to consume them at his leisure. He was said to be over thirty feet long, his belly wider than a dinghy, and his head so immense that it could swallow down a whole "Barra" boar.

During his reign, some of the finest croc shooters in the North pitted their wits against his in a futile effort to secure the ultimate trophy. By the 1980s professional and sports fishermen, along with local farmers, were complaining to the department of National Parks and Wildlife that this crocodile was a menace. They felt threatened by his presence and wanted him destroyed or removed.

The government sent in professional crocodile catchers who worked for crocodile farms to rid the area of any crocodiles deemed dangerous, but the big black croc's instincts allowed him to avoid capture easily. Man was his only fear, but he'd learned about man, the invaders of his territory who were torturing and taking his girls when the tranquil still of night was disturbed by the thundering of outboard motors and by piercing bright lights. They had been killing his family for over fifty years and he knew that if he looked at the lights, the loudest of all animals would call and his death would follow.

It was in 1985, while assisting the Queensland National Parks and Wildlife Service with relocating rogue crocodiles, that Dad and I heard the tale of this legendary croc. We felt drawn to him.

In 1987 we surveyed the croc's territory and in 1988 we had been designated caretakers of his river system. We were to work under the East Coast Crocodile Management Program, set up by the Queensland National Parks and Wildlife Service, and our objective was to remove and relocate rogue or problem crocs from populated areas.

Typical freshwater croc habitat.

My family felt that our participation in the croc management program was the best way to protect the crocs from humans. Our aim was to catch and relocate them before they made the mistake of showing themselves around populated areas.

From the moment Dad and I laid eyes on the habitat belonging to the big croc we fell in love with it, a

truly magnificent tidal system laced with enchanted mangroves and wetlands fed by the spectacular tropical rainforests of the Great Dividing Range. This picturesque environment supported a myriad of wildlife, from its apex predator, the saltwater

Crocodile slide on a tidal mud bank.

crocodile, to docile vegetarians, from agile wallabies to microscopic marine life.

But the area is the scene of classic conflict between man and the environment. Cane farms are bulldozed all the way to the river, and there's pollution of the river systems exacerbated by speed boats.

We spent many months scanning the muddy riverbanks, a primeval ooze teeming with life, on the low tides, hoping to see the slides or marks left by our quarry. Countless lead-in baits, lures, and traps were set to no avail.

Then, one morning, Dad spotted our first sign. The big black croc had made a mistake. Dad located a belly slide tucked up in the mangroves where the big old fella had spent some time basking the previous day.

Several days later, Dad left me, with faithful dog Chilli, in the croc's territory. One man and one dog in the vast maze of mangroves, pitted against the legend. I set two traps in the vicinity of the belly slide Dad had located. Then I set my biggest trap upstream from the belly slide, in the area I considered the wildlife "hot spot," the stretch of the river prolific with wallabies, pigs, flying fox, fish, and mudcrabs: perfect croc cuisine.

Another trap was set down toward the mouth of the river in the area where the majority of "man versus beast" stories originated. The mouth of a river is of prime importance in a large male's

It was hard work preparing a trap site.

assertion of dominance in his territory. This old bloke would have had many bone-crunching fights with subordinate males trying to cut in on his turf.

Every time I entered his part of the river I could feel his presence. Often in the stillness of the night I'd cut the outboard, turn on the spotlight, and drift. And every time an eerie sensation would overwhelm me. Even Chilli could sense it. My task was awesome and, by crikey, I was going to be careful!

One night I spotted the eyeshine of a small croc, about ten feet long, which I assumed was one of the croc's girls. I quickly unraveled a net, tied it to the mangroves, then reversed out into the middle of the river, hoping the current from the tide would drift the net around the croc. Briefly turning on my spotty, I picked up her eyeshine. The net was coming around nicely. Another scan with the spotty: the crocodile was coming straight for me, against the current! Adrenaline surged, and my hands were sweating and shaking so hard I couldn't start the outboard. I was panicking.

"Stevo, slow down! Slow down!" I kept repeating, trying to get the grip on myself I needed. "Chilli, get in the middle of the boat and stay!" I commanded. I grabbed the spotlight. It had been disconnected by my scared little dog.

Scrambling frantically, I reconnected the spotty. Confidence was regained once I had the power of light in my hands. I scanned the river. There it was. The net was now past my boat and heading upstream at a good rate of knots.

"Start the outboard!" I had to shout at myself for my body to react. The boat caught up to the trailing ends of the net. "C'mon, Stevo . . . think, boy, think."

The floats upstream were disappearing, the net was being dragged under. Scurrying to the bow of the boat, I grabbed the net ends and tied them to the bow hook. I jumped back toward the outboard as an almighty surge pulled the bow of my boat underwater. Regaining an even keel, I slammed the idling outboard into reverse.

"Back off, Steve! Back off!"

The reverse thrust of the outboard against the "nuclear sub" I'd caught in the net pulled the bow under and I began to take in water.

"Crikey, I'm going to sink! Forward, forward! Get into forward!"

Acco attacks! He's a little cranky!

Before I had the presence of mind to jam the motor into forward gear, the bow sprang back out of the water like a slingshot. Seconds later the net floated up and drifted back toward the boat. Apprehensively I gathered the net and headed back to camp. There was a hole in the net that you could have driven a 4WD through. *Whew!* Thank God for that.

It seemed obvious that old legend, the big black croc, had been sidling up to one of his girls at the time, so he had challenged the net, perhaps in her defense. The ease with which the mighty dinosaur ripped through the net was proof of an animal with intense power.

My second encounter with the old legend occurred another day around dusk. Chilli and I were in hot pursuit of a group of feral pigs which, to get the drop on us, had decided to swim for it. They quickly entered the water and headed toward the opposite bank—almost seven hundred feet away. Out of breath, I hastily grabbed Chilli before she swam after them—the staffie (Staffordshire) in her seemed to cloud her common sense. This stretch of river belonged to the legend and I'm sure he'd love to eat my little dog.

We sat on the bank and excitedly watched the pigs swim to the other bank, hoping the legend would emerge and strike at one of the porkers. Four, and then five, reached the bank, and boggingly climbed the muddy incline. The last pig reached the bank, dug its front hooves into the mud to pull itself up, but then slid backward and simply disappeared back into the water. No squeals, no thrashing, it just disappeared beneath the swirling river. The other pigs didn't notice one was missing and wouldn't be scared crossing this part of the river in the future, thus ensuring the big croc of a steady food supply.

I hung around for an hour, hoping to see the croc emerge with the porker in his jaws and swallow it down, but it was not to be. Days flowed into weeks, then months. Still no sign of the big fella coming anywhere near my traps. Not one lead-in bait had been touched.

Chilli and I had become part of the mangroves; birds and wallabies accepted us as part of their everyday life. My stalking skills became very refined. Sometimes I'd squat for hours in the insect-infested mangroves, camouflaged with leaves and mud, just hoping to glimpse my target crocodile. But nothing, not one thing. I was starting to lose the plot— I calculated that it was over eighteen months since I'd first anticipated catching this elusive old croc.

Then at the cracka one morning I was doing my routine trap run when I noticed a lead-in bait had gone. Excitedly I jammed the boat into the mangroves and

One of the traps I set up to catch Acco, this one up near the mouth of the river in the spectacular wetland habitat of North Queensland where this big croc lived.

grabbed the bait's nylon cord. It had been pulled so hard it had been flung up into the branches, severed by a large downward force. The entire fist-sized piece of fresh pork and part of the nylon cord were gone. Was this the croc's second mistake? I was so excited I didn't even swat the ants biting my eyelids. It was the trap I'd anticipated he'd hit, my biggest trap in the wildlife "hot spot."

You beauty!

That day Chilli and I got a fairly large putrid piece of meat to use in re-baiting the trap. I parked my boat way downstream and carried the bait in over my shoulder. This way I would leave no tracks or boat disturbance around the entrance to the trap. Surely the rotting meat would be enticing to him.

That night I couldn't sleep. It took forever for the sun to appear. First light I raced straight to the trap. Nothing. Nothing touched, no signs, no slides, no marks—nothing. Just bloody green ants. Disappointed and a little grumpy, I muttered to Chilli, "It's cool. It's always four nights after they've hit the lead-in. Remember your own observations."

The next night came around; it was a struggle to sleep. Next morning, nothing at the traps. The following night it was easier to sleep—the excitement was dwindling. Sure enough, next morning nothing again at the traps.

That day Chilli and I lugged in a huge Barra boar, which I carefully placed in the "hot spot" trap, hoping its smell would do the trick.

Mysteriously, that night I was abruptly woken by a commotion in the mangroves. Something was wrong. Chilli was alert and agitated, the klunk klunk bird was silent, and the fireflies were thick. It was a few more hours until daylight, so I stoked up the campfire and dozed, engulfed by the warmth of the blaze.

At first light Chilli and I casually fueled up and headed for the traps. It was different on the river this morning. Nothing at the first couple of traps. As I rounded the bend and zoomed into the "hot spot" trap, I got the shock of my life. Adrenaline surged through my swollen veins. "This is it, Chilli! This is it! Stay cool, Steve."

The mangroves erupted; a huge jolting force pounded the bow of the boat. Panic was pushing my eyeballs out—I must stay in control! Oh crikey! His tail and back leg are out of the trap—my trap's not big enough! The tide's coming in and already he's surrounded by water. Think quick! Keep a grip . . . get a top-jaw rope.

Securing the boat in the trap entrance, I climbed into the mangroves with a couple of top-jaw ropes and headed in toward the croc's head. *Whack!* As soon as he saw me he head-butted a huge mangrove tree and snapped it off.

"Settle, boy, settle!"

Whack! He clobbered another huge tree. Once around the front of his head, I snapped off a stick and tried to thread a top-jaw rope between his massive yellow teeth. He lunged straight at me, ripping the stick and rope clean out of my hands. He snorted and blew mucus and spray into my face. His eyes were wide, full of anger and fear.

"Chilli! Get around here!" But no way was she budging from the safety of the boat.

Whoosh! The croc exploded in a thrashing frenzy. He gripped the trap in his teeth and went into a series of violent death rolls. The instant he stopped I positioned my top-jaw rope

Me and a local bloke with an adult female saltwater crocodile I captured in the eighties.

stick, then jammed it between those huge teeth and pushed it out the other side. Scampering between the aerial mangrove roots, I seized the rope end before he had time to react. I sensed he was tired.

"You're a big boy, you're a monster . . . but are you the legend?" As I talked to him constantly, he hissed and growled straight back at me.

Finally I secured my first top-jaw rope and hastily knotted it to the nearest tree. I readied another rope. As soon as I was in range to secure it he exploded again. He struck out at me with a bone-crunching head thrash, then spun into another death roll. This time the jaw rope wrapped around his head, and the tree it was tied to was winched down until it snapped off. He

Being captured and crated was undoubtedly traumatic for this big croc but it saved his life.

settled and I regained the rope and secured it to the biggest tree in the vicinity. Hoping it would hold, I secured another two top-jaw ropes while he re-covered.

I felt no fear; I was working on in-stinct. Sheer guts and determination were stamped in my brain.

Now that he was restrained, I had to shift him. I climbed back into the boat, grabbed a trap and bags, and threw them over his head, which worked as a blindfold.

Happy that he was temporarily secured, I sped back to my camp and grabbed my back-up boat and a winch. The moment I returned he violently shook and death rolled, but my jaw rope held strong. As I pushed the back-up boat alongside him I was reminded of the speed with which the tide was coming in.

I'm running out of time, I thought. In the trap he'll drown quickly on the high tide.

His breaths were deep and drawn out—he was exhausted. Within minutes I'd secured the winch to the trap and commenced winching. The slack was taking up nicely. Then he exploded into another death roll. Both trees I was winching from snapped off and fell straight on his back, followed by me and the winch. He growled and thrashed. Thank God my jaw ropes held.

It appeared impossible that just one person would be able to manipulate such an awesome, powerful mass into the boat. I pondered for a moment. The croc hissed and started into another death roll and I lurched the boat on its side as he rolled. His massive body engulfed the boat and rolled it upright. Incredibly, he was in the boat. Quickly I ran ropes around the entire croc and boat, hoping to restrain him in the flimsy dinghy.

Once I was happy he was secured to the boat, the reality hit me: I'm going to need help. The tide was powering in and it was obvious that croc and boat were not going to float. At a great rate of knots I got back to camp, jumped into my 4WD, drove to the nearest homestead, and alerted some locals.

When we got to the trap my helpers were overwhelmed by fear. Although the croc was secured in a boat—which was now underwater—it took some real persuasion and ten cartons of beer to get them to help. The tide was almost high and the boat was completely submerged but luckily the croc's nostrils were above the water. Eight burly farmers and myself were only just force enough to lift the boat and croc up out of the water sufficiently to allow us to bail out the water. With a boat on each side of the black bloke and me in with him bailing out water, we kept him afloat and got him back to a nearby ramp on a cattle property. The owner obligingly got his front-end loader and we lifted croc and boat from the ramp onto dry land.

A crowd started to develop. News of the "legend's" capture traveled like wildfire. I walked in circles, torn between success and despair. Had I done the right thing? Would this truly magnificent ruler have eventually succumbed to the shooters otherwise? Was my intervention right or wrong?

People shook my hand, patted my back. I wasn't a hero; I just loved my crocs and would do anything to protect them.

Acco today, at home in the Park.

The situation's not their fault, it's people's. Surely we can learn to live with them. This bloke's not an enemy—he's a king.

"Please get back from him, move back," I pleaded. The onlookers were starting to make me angry.

"Oh, he's so ugly . . ."

"There's a few good boots, bags, and belts in this one . . ."

"You should shoot the lot of 'em . . ."

Such were the saddening comments flowing from their mouths.

Luckily some people from the National Parks and Wildlife Service arrived with a crate. The exhausted old croc, blindfolded and confused, was slowly winched into the crate. He managed enough strength to deliver a final death roll, defiant to the end. Tears trickled down my cheeks.

"Please don't die," I whispered to him.

After being crated, he was sent down to our park by rail. Dad met him at the railway station and immediately flew into action. He had him in his new territory with a beautiful girlfriend within an hour. Dad understood the stress this poor old croc was suffering and cut no corners to ensure that he was treated like royalty.

Back at camp I was sitting by the campfire, cuddling Chilli, feeling empty and fearful for the croc's life. The capture of the big black legend was going to change him and me for the rest of our lives.

Chapter III

Out West, a Wide Brown Land

The world's most venomous snake, the fierce snake (or western taipan), with venom fifty times more toxic than the Indian cobra, produces enough toxins in one bite to kill dozens of healthy adult humans. Discovered and described in the 1870s, this Australian species was then unseen by scientists for nearly one hundred years. The place in which it was rediscovered in 1972 is an area close to my heart and one that I still frequently visit to conduct scientific research.

The desire to find the fierce snake stimulated a massive effort by the Queensland Museum and Dad and myself, and it was during this hunt that my passion for the deserts, plains, and escarpments of Central Australia was kindled.

We've always referred to Central Australia as "out west." As the crow flies it's approximately seven hundred miles due-west of the Reptile Park. Even as a kid I remember the relentless, never-ending drive to get there. It usually takes twenty-four hours of straight driving on a good run—the conditions become more extreme the further west you go. Central Australia

My ground-level approach to studying fierce snakes.

is a land of graphic contrasts. Drought one day, floods the next. From scorchingly unbearable heat to freezing cold. And then there's the dust and flies.

After a few days of scorching heat the wind will build to gale force, picking up dirt and sand in its path and blowing it across the landscape. Once, Dad and I were struck by a dust storm in which visibility was down to thirty feet; even our 4WD was penetrated by clouds of powder-like dust. When the dust storms pass, on come the flies. These sticky little black bush flies have driven many unseasoned travelers insane. Basically, you've got to handle being subjected to having a swarm of writhing flies all over your body from sunup to sundown.

But I guess it's the heat that sorts out the men from the boys in this country. Twenty-four hours without water in the summer heat and you're dead. If your vehicle breaks down out here you're instantly in loads of trouble. Even on the busier roads you may see only a couple of cars in a week. On the more remote tracks you may only see a vehicle once or twice a year. The harsh arid interior of Australia is no place for the pampered or foolhardy. It's a rugged land worked by rugged blokes and their families.

Fierce snake: the world's most venomous snake.

All of the animals that live out in the west have, of course, adapted to the hot, dry conditions, and although it often looks like an extremely dry, desolate, lifeless landscape, it's actually teeming with a myriad of wildlife. Each new day the cool morning air rings to a crescendo of bird calls. As the day warms up, hawks and eagles begin to circle in the thermals while lizards bask on rocks. The land's nocturnal marsupials, pythons, and owls sleep soundly in their cool retreats.

When looking at this habitat, it's easy to see why the fierce snake "disappeared" for so long. The area where the species lives, Ashy Downs, or the Black Soil Plains of Central Australia, is treeless and arid, and the snake survives the extremes and harshness of its surrounds by living

Drought one day, floods the next; Central Australia is a land of contrast.

underground. Beneath the dry bare dirt of the plains is a subterranean labyrinth of cracks and rat holes.

The fierce snake doesn't often venture outside, waiting until there is very little wind and dust, usually coming to the surface in the mornings between seven and ten o'clock when the temperature is a "cool" 32°C (90°F). Once it heats up over 90°F the snakes slither back underground to the safety of their holes. Unless the climate and conditions are perfect you'll never see a snake, not even a scale. When Dad and I first searched, many days went by before we spotted our first fierce snake—and then it got away.

My boyhood memories of this wide brown land start with a grazier's homestead nearly two hundred miles from Birdsville. The graziers, Herb and Pearl, were our good mates, and Dad and I would religiously call in to the homestead for the traditional "cuppa" and a "yarn." These people were the salt of the earth and they loved the land and its wildlife.

At night, we'd sit around a campfire and I'd listen in awe to Herb's yarns of the deepest

Piggy Wig. He was like the homestead watchdog.

floods, the longest droughts, the biggest fierce snakes, the rarest mammals, and the harshest dust storms. We got on like a house on fire. But whenever I visited Herb and Pearl's, I'd always be looking behind me. They had a pet feral pig named Piggy Wig which they'd raised from a porker. He was like the homestead watchdog and, unfortunately, he didn't like me or Dad. I got bitten once before I learned to give him a wide berth and respect his space.

One time I was scratching around the machinery shed chasing lizards when Piggy Wig decided he didn't want me near his shed, so he commenced grunting his way toward me. I quickly shot up onto a bulldozer blade, where I sat in the scorching heat for a couple of hours, too scared to move. Once he'd put me up on the blade he waddled off a short distance into the shade for a dust-bath and a rest, waiting for me to come down. Not even the heat or my thirst convinced me to make a run for it. I was totally parched by the time Herb casually came to the rescue.

Most of the cattle properties out west are as large as some small countries. Herb was a keen pilot and used his small plane to cover the distances quickly and to muster his cattle. I loved flying with Herb, and it was during these flights as a boy that I gained an understanding of the lay of the land and just how vast and arid it is.

Dad's Toyota Landcruiser, set up as an all-terrain snake-catching machine.

But chasing snakes was our mission! Not just any old venomous snake, but the most venomous snake in the world. Dad's Toyota Landcruiser 4WD was an all-terrain, snake-catching machine, fully rigged with all the essential gear.

Tracks in the sand—evidence of sand goannas.

We often camped back in the red sand dune country. The red sand dunes of Central Australia are a wonder of the world; they're shaped by the winds and run in parallel lines often miles long. Imagine the fun I had playing and chasing lizards in this never-ending sandpit. I'd dive off the steepest edges then roll all the way to the bottom. What a thrill! Even Dad had a go—in a weaker moment, I should add.

Tracking was my greatest achievement. I could track in the sand, often catching and releasing a hundred lizards in an hour. One afternoon I tracked this huge sand goanna that had raided our camp while we were out chasing snakes. He led me nearly three-quarters of a mile through the bright orange-red sand, over four sand dunes, across a clay pan, and right up to his den—a perfect tunnel down to the moist, cool clay beneath the sand dune. I was sitting at the entrance waiting in ambush when I spotted fresh bird tracks . . . big bird tracks, the middle toe longer than my footprint—emus! So off I went tracking fresh emu tracks.

Heading into the huge orange glow of the west's glorious, lengthy sunset, I was thinking to myself how fresh the tracks were and that I must be close. Sure enough, when I reached the knife-edged crest of an eighty-foot sand dune, there they were, catching grasshoppers in the spinifex at the base of a truly spectacular sand dune. Pulling out my grandfather's binoculars, I focused on the seven flightless giants. I was intrigued by how many grasshoppers they were eating, and how the younger ones puffed out their chests and pranced around or ran at each other. I desperately yearned to go down and play with them but I'd learned valuable lessons about not approaching wildlife without purpose. Besides, it was an experience I couldn't wait to get back and tell Dad about.

The perentie is another of the fascinating creatures living in this rugged landscape.

I ran like the wind, back-tracking toward camp. By the time I got to the last sand dune, I could see the 4WD and the glow of the fire—just across from the biggest fire of them all. The sun was like a giant orange fireball touching the horizon. The ripples in the sand were now patterned with shadows and, as I changed pace to a slow idle, a knob-tailed gecko shot across

My photo of the knob-tailed gecko, taken in red-dune country.

my foot into a spinifex clump. It was too dark to be fossicking around without a torch so I marked the clump with a stick so I could find it later.

"How'd ya go, son?" Dad asked, as I got within earshot of camp. "You've been gone for hours."

"Wow, great! I saw heaps—plenty of dragons, a flock of emus, tracked a big sandy, and I nearly stood on a knobby!" I replied.

"A knob-tailed gecko? When?"

"It was just up there five minutes ago."

"I'll grab the torches, you grab the camera," Dad said. "Do you think you can find the spot again?"

"Yeah, no worries. It's up here."

No sooner had I spotted my marker stick when Dad said, "Look, son, there he is—near these sticks. See if you can sneak in for a shot. I'll keep him right on the edge of my beam."

Without uttering a word, I stealthily crawled around Dad's knees, flicked on the flash, and snapped off some of my most treasured photographs. We watched the gecko go about

Flooded plains mean the end of this road anyway.

his business for a few minutes, then charged back to camp, jumped in the 4WD, and went spotlighting for snakes and looking at the nocturnal mammals and owls.

It was a great night's spotting. We saw red kangaroos and dingoes, hopping mice out on the plains, an owl feeding on a rat, and plenty of snakes and geckos in between. I was asleep before we made it back to camp, so tired I don't remember getting into my swag.

During the night, Dad had decided to try searching for fierce snakes further north. We packed up camp at first light and were heading toward the Black Soil Plains when Dad commented on the ominous-looking black clouds.

"It doesn't rain out here much, lad, but when it does we don't want to be anywhere near."

Dad decided we'd better head for higher ground and the nearest bitumen road.

The rain started slowly—there seemed to be more wind than rain—but it was enough to turn the bull dust to grease and the ground to bog. Dad dropped the 4WD back to high-range second gear to minimize the sliding. Many times we went into a slide, heading down the road sideways or even backward.

As the thirsty landscape soaked up the light, steady rain, the sliding problem

Hatching fierce snake eggs.

diminished as we sank deeper and deeper into the grease-like mud. This was the ultimate test for any 4WD and driver. Dad was down to low-range 4WD and had to rev the engine to the red line, and hold it for hundreds of yards at a time. The engine peaked so hard for so long that it pinged and missed. It took us four hours to do four miles. Every mile we had to stop and chisel out the incredibly tacky mud that had built up between the wheels and the chassis. Our 4WD had worked so hard that the mud compacted around the wheels was hot. When we hit water, steam came off the setting mud pack.

We struggled all day to finally reach the bitumen; when we did, Dad immediately pulled over and made a cuppa in the rain. Due to the real threat of being bogged out in the

Australia's largest lizard, the perentie.

sand dunes for a month, we hadn't dared to stop for a drink or a feed. Dad's a devoted teetotaller and his driving force to get to the safety of the bitumen was a cuppa.

Central Australia—truly a land of great beauty.

The hardships of traversing this dramatically changing landscape are insignificant when compared to the beauty of the wilderness and the wildlife experiences. My love for this land has drawn me back time and time again over the last twenty-five years.

Together, Terri and I passionately

explore and research this thirsty, rugged landscape. We're currently conducting research on the fierce snake and the perentie. It's been a real thrill teaching Terri stress-free techniques to restrain the number-one most venomous snake in the world. The snakes aren't too stressed but Terri sweats buckets she's so nervous. She's the only sheila I know who's capable of tossing the deadliest of snakes. We have an absolute ball out there and are producing some major scientific data, which eventually we hope to utilize to conserve this fragile, hot environment and its fascinating wildlife.

Terri chases down another fierce snake for capture.

Chapter IV

Getting Agro

After a three-week stint in the bush without seeing or hearing another human, I was a little excited to see the nearest telephone box. This was the late 1980s and I was working full-time catching rogue crocs for the Queensland National Parks and Wildlife Service. It was nearly twenty miles by 4WD to the nearest civilization and phone.

"Gidday, Dad, how are ya?" I greeted him excitedly.

"Not bad, son, howze it all goin' up there?"

"Yeah, really good, thanks. I've got eight traps set between Townsville and Cairns, the two crocs near Townsville are just starting to hit the lead-in baits. Spotted that little fella at the main boat ramp. He let me get within a few feet, so we can jump him whenever I get some back-up. When are you coming up?" I asked.

"I can't go anywhere, so you're on your own for another couple of months," Dad explained. "Can't a National Parks and Wildlife Service bloke back you up and drive the boat so you can jump that little fella? They seem really keen to get it captured before some idiot shoots it first."

"Yeah, it's a real worry," I replied. "I was talking to the local fishermen on the weekend and they've already taken matters into their own hands and tried to kill it. They reckon it's in excess of eleven feet and that it's been stalking their kids. They must've been seeing its back and head while it was in the water and mistaken it for a larger crocodile head.

"It's a real popular ramp, probably one hundred fifty to two hundred people down there every weekend, so I reckon its days are numbered. I'll get right onto it. What else is news?"

"Well, lad, I just got told by the National Parks powers-that-be that the notorious big male croc near the S-bend is back again and he's popping up right alongside people in boats. He's gotta come out before he gets too bold for his own good. That's the fourth recent complaint about him so you better get onto him. Have you got any large traps available?" Dad asked with a sense of urgency.

"Yep," I replied, "I've got the big blue one and a black trap sitting at camp ready for action."

"Good. You'll see a piece of silver duct tape in the mangroves where I spotted him last. It looks like the likeliest location for a trap—right on the shallow bend where the high tide goes up into the mangroves," Dad explained.

"Yeah, Dad, I know the spot well. I'm surprised that naughty croc is still alive—apparently he's got a bad habit of sitting under the shade of the mangroves and staring at people fishing. He seems to have a territory over a mile long, and at least one eight-foot female occasionally suns herself with him. I reckon he'll be an easy croc to trap as he's got a pretty aggressive air about him."

"You be careful, son. I know for a fact this croc's got a real attitude problem. When I surveyed his territory I could feel his presence the whole time. He's really bold and isn't scared to mix it up with bigger males. This is one croc I'd consider as a potential threat. Don't take any risks or your mother will kill me. She's right off the idea of you tossing it on your own."

"Yeah, Dad. It's not a problem."

Agro territory.

"Don't get me wrong," Dad added jokingly, "*I'm* not the slightest bit worried about you. It's your mother that's got me shaking in me boots."

"I'll be careful and I'll give you a ring as soon as I've jumped the little fella or caught this agro croc," I said confidently. "If I don't have any luck I'll give you a call in about two weeks. I should've run out of fuel about then and will have to come into town anyway."

"OK, mate! Take it steady. I'll talk to you soon," he replied with concern.

"See ya, Dad!" I shouted as I hung up the phone.

Once I'd filled my jerry cans with outboard fuel and diesel for my 4WD, I loaded up with some bare essential groceries and headed back to my camp. Along the way I was daydreaming, pondering the plight of the saltwater crocodile. Almost driving on automatic pilot, my mind was a million miles away, trying to picture what this land was like before mankind came along, and wondering if Australians and visitors to Australia will ever become proud of the largest reptile on the planet.

Up until the early 1970s crocodile shooting was legal. Crocs were regarded as a pest and countless thousands of them were shot for their belly skins. Crocodiles were considered fair game and were also shot for sport and trophies.

We should be *proud* of our crocodiles. Here in Australia we don't have large predatory mammals such as lions, tigers, or bears; no, we're in the land of the reptile. The crocodiles are ancient animals dating back sixty-five million years. Today, virtually unchanged, they are modern-day dinosaurs. They're certainly the kings of Australian fauna.

Before the arrival of modern man, crocodiles were common from Northern Australia up to Papua New Guinea and Indonesia, through the Malay Peninsula into Thailand and the Bay of Bengal. The wholesale slaughter of crocs since has pushed them to the brink of extinction throughout the majority of their range. It's only in the Northern Australian region that their numbers can be considered stable.

Once upon a time these large saurians ruled the waterways, with adult animals having no natural predators except larger, more dominant crocodiles. There was no such thing as an over-population of crocs; their intricate social structure and the availability of food kept their numbers in check. It is we humans who have introduced conflict and a breakdown of their social structure. The en-

A 9 1/2 foot saltwater crocodile that Agro killed.

croachment of civilization has been a detriment to our entire northern ecosystem's stability and health.

Capturing an adult saltwater crocodile for relocation.

The saltwater crocodile is the number one species in the food chain. It is the apex predator and wherever there remains a natural habitat and healthy croc numbers you'll find wildlife "hot spots" of great biological diversity and flourishing populations of all species. Unfortunately there are few wilderness areas that support such healthy crocodile populations.

The problem we face—and one that our children's children will continue to face—is the lack of harmonious coexistence between humans and large predators. Whether it's a great white shark, a Bengal tiger, a grizzly bear, or a saltwater croc, if someone gets attacked it's the animal that suffers. For example, in 1985 a middle-aged woman decided to go for a swim at night in known crocodile territory and was killed and consumed by a croc measuring over fourteen feet. The week after her death, over two hundred crocodiles, both large and small, were killed by vigilantes and locals seeking revenge.

It is this sort of slaughter and unwarranted hatred that has become my driving force. If I don't capture problem crocs and alleviate the potential conflict, the entire ecosystem will corrode from the removal of the apex predator.

Once I'd reached my camp on a salt flat in the mangroves, I wasted no time loading up my dinghy with the black trap and gear. It was serene and tranquil motoring along the river looking for croc tracks and slides. Within an hour I'd located a couple of fresh slides in the deep mud where a croc of approximately twelve feet had dragged itself out of the water to sunbake earlier in the morning. Like all reptiles the crocodile is poikilothermal, or, as they are often misleadingly known, "cold-blooded." Rather, reptiles utilize the temperature of the sun, air, and water to govern their body temperature. Their optimum temperature is approximately 30°C, or 86°F, and if they're feeling a little cool they'll climb up the muddy banks to sunbake in a patch of sun to warm up. This activity

Scouting locations for setting traps can be tough work.

provides me with a positive identification of the croc's mass, its territorial limits, and a general idea of its daily routine.

Restraining this 9 1/2 foot saltwater crocodile (male) is no easy task.

I located the silver duct tape Dad had stuck to a mangrove branch. He was dead right—this was the center of the croc's territory and an ideal location to set the trap.

The tide was low and on the rise. Nosing the boat into the grassy mud, I saw I'd have to carry the trapping gear twenty feet up to the mangroves to set up the trap. Always a little on edge, I had a cursory look around to make sure I wasn't going to jump straight out of the boat into an ambush. Everything seemed settled and tranquil so I tossed out the trap, axe, shovel, bags, and ropes. They partially sank in the mud. As I lowered myself out of the boat I quickly sank up to my waist in the ooze that literally teems with small bugs and mud skippers. I felt more than usually vulnerable: I was close to the murky water's edge and would have no hope of movement in the retarding mud if the croc had wanted me for lunch.

"Stay in the boat," I ordered my best mate, Chilli. She was much safer there and I couldn't afford to have her scurrying around attracting the attention of a hungry croc.

I was vulnerable enough. Crocs love to eat dogs; they must taste great.

I've learned the hard way to rely on my instincts, and while I trudged toward the mangroves my instincts were working overtime. It took me three lengthy, strenuous trips to carry the gear to the trap site. I was well aware of the commotion I was creating and my senses were telling me not to drop my guard.

"Use your instincts, Stevo, use your instincts," I kept muttering to myself as I finally got all the trap gear into the mass of twisting mangrove roots.

Pulling my knife, I started clearing the site. The weight of the long blade felt good in my hand; it became an extension of my arm. Sweat poured from my body as I positioned the trap and tied it off. An hour slipped away. I was transfixed with work, contemplating the arduous task of hauling the mud bag twenty feet up into the mangrove branches, when I realized the tide had crept up to my site.

Repositioning the boat so it was between me and the ever-deepening water, I cautioned Chilli to stay in the boat. She just sat there watching my every move with ever-adoring eyes.

"Now comes the hard part," I told her.

I climbed up an overhanging mangrove tree to a good solid fork and began struggling and straining; inch by inch I hauled up the heavy weight bag. With it secured for the moment, I climbed down to the trap. The incoming tide was now covering the floor of the trap. Better move quick or I'll be working underwater, I thought.

While tying off the strings that support the trap, I watched the water rushing in. The boat swung out into the increasing tidal current, and as the water rose above my knees, the sun was starting to set.

I turned away from the deep water to secure the last of the strings when an overwhelming sensation of being stalked stopped me in my tracks. Quickly I turned to face the water.

"Knock it off, Stevo, you're spooking yourself," I said, trying to reassure myself there was no danger and fighting the fear.

I turned to finish my job when Chilli let out an almighty scream. I didn't turn to look—I grabbed at the mangroves and pulled myself into the branches, waiting for the thump of jaw pressure hitting my body. I scrambled higher and higher. Safe in the fork of the tree with the weight bag, I relaxed and took a look.

Nothing. I could see nothing. Chilli was going ballistic, barking aggressively at the water below the boat.

Another close call.

"It's OK, girl," I called out. "There's nothing there!"

Bang! The boat jerked at a force that hit from below so hard that Chilli fell onto the floor. She regained her posture and continued to bark frantically at the water. A huge swirl churned the muddy waters.

Thump! Again something bumped the bottom of the boat, making it jerk as if it had run aground. Helplessly stuck in the tree, I beckoned Chilli to settle down. She wouldn't, no way. *Bark, bark, bark, bark!*

"Dad! Dad! There's a croc under the boat!" she was screaming in dog language.

"I know, sweetheart. Settle down, pull your head in," I pleaded with her. "Please, Chilli! Sit, babe, sit." I was sure that before my eyes the croc was going to explode from the murk and pull her out of the boat by her head.

Knowing I would take a hit if I climbed down and went for the boat, I located a long branch and swiftly sliced through it with my knife, stripping off the leaves and twigs. Chilli continued to bark so hard she was going off the Richter scale.

I struck out at my boat with the stick, but it was too short. My life depending on stealth and accuracy, I climbed down toward the water. Again I struck out with the stick, this time catching the side of the bow just enough to get purchase and draw the boat toward me.

With the boat directly under me again, I pulled out my knife and jumped straight into the boat. Jarring my ankles on impact, I raised my razor-like blade and in one slice cut the anchor rope, swung at the outboard, and fired it up with one pull. Thank goodness! I jammed it into reverse and gunned it.

Feeling secure in the boat, I slowed in the middle of the river, keeping the motor idling. I stared at the water immediately in front of the trap site. Nothing, not even a swirl. Whew! Dad's right, this croc has got one hell of an attitude. Confident the croc was being intimidated by the magnified thump of the idling outboard motor, I cruised back in toward the trap.

All was quiet, almost peaceful. Had it been our imagination, or not? No way, I thought, cuddling Chilli in an embrace of thanks and love. I reckon she'd saved my life, but it wasn't until the next morning when I returned to the trap site that I fully understood what had taken place. With the mud exposed on the low tide, the evidence was graphic. Two huge footprints were embedded in the mud where the croc had poised, ready to strike.

Later, as I planned the safest strategy for baiting the trap, I sliced off a piece of fresh meat and then I jumped over the bow and into the mud. Backward, I trudged toward the trap, never taking my eyes off the water.

At the trap entrance I had to crawl up inside the trap to set the bait. Once set, I wasted no time in grabbing my rifle and retreating to the safety of my boat. I cut off another nice, juicy piece of meat, attached it to a strong nylon cord, and positioned it so that it dangled over the front of the trap. This lead-in bait was an irresistible bite-sized morsel of fresh meat to lure the croc that night.

Firing up the outboard, I swung the boat around and headed back to camp. Once at the boat ramp, I pulled my boat out of the water and loaded it onto the trailer. Later that night I was going to use the boat elsewhere, having a go at the little fella down at the main boat ramp.

Arriving at the ramp just on dark, I wasted no time getting the boat in and the equipment organized. Luckily, the boat ramp was deserted, which meant there'd be little or no disturbance from boat traffic. I connected the

A hindquarter of pig makes an enticing lead-in bait. Once a crocodile takes the lead-in bait it's only a matter of time before it will go for the bait in the trap.

spotties and had a quick check around. *Whammo!* Eyeshine! Not twenty feet off the end of the concrete boat ramp.

"Gee! You're a cocky little croc," I said, wondering how the little blighter had avoided being shot.

Firing up the outboard and reversing into midstream, I wondered how I was going to jump this croc without somebody driving the boat or backing me up. Jumping crocs at night requires a minimum of two experienced people. Well, there was just me and my dog!

Deciding on a technique that I'd only just thought of, I raised the spotty and, sure enough, the croc was sitting in the deep water out from the ramp—with only eyes and nose exposed above the water level. Crocs will sit with only the three points out of the water with their body angled down at forty-five degrees, so they can submerge or shoot forward quickly using their webbed feet and strong paddle-like tails. The trick is to spear yourself right at them and hope you get them around the neck before they pull away. If you grab the croc too far forward or back, it'll simply swing round and bite down. Accuracy and timing is the name of the game.

Crocs sit with only three points out of the water.

Jamming the outboard into forward gear, I idled directly toward the bright red glow of the smallish croc's eyes, spotty in one hand and driving the boat with the other. When I got to within ten feet from the croc it slowly paddled toward the mangroves. I could now tell by its head size that it was a jumpable size.

The gap narrowed; closer and closer I crept. Before the eyeshine dipped below the level of the bow, I released the outboard and strode to the bow. The boat, still in forward gear, was headed right at the croc. I braced, dug my toes in, and speared straight at the croc, dropping the spotty mid-flight into the water.

Hit. My hands made contact, I gripped down hard and I desperately tried to secure the croc's tail with my legs. I couldn't. I'd missed the neck and had it mid-body. Thrashing violently, the croc took me down to the bottom between the mangrove roots. Feeling that it couldn't shake me, it thrashed around with its bony head, smashing into my cheekbone. Releasing a hand, I grabbed at its head, and my fingers went straight in its mouth! As the croc bit down I released my other hand and grabbed its head. It had me and I had it!

Pulling it tight into my body to stop its thrashing, I secured the croc's rear end with my inner thighs. The croc was starting to subdue as Dad's famous words went through my mind: "If a croc's biting you, you'll know you've got him!"

Now desperate for air, I pushed off a mangrove root for the surface, and suddenly my head slammed into the muddy bottom. I was upside-down! Again I pushed up for the surface. Yes! I broke through to the air and sucked in a lungful.

Although four of my fingers were jammed in the croc's jaws, I didn't dare release my grip on its head. Peering through the dark, I couldn't see my boat, but I could hear it in the distance still motoring.

"Bugger it!"

Not able to release my grip to swim for the bank, I exhaled and sank back to the muddy bottom. The little croc thrashed again and tried for a death roll but I was easily able to keep it subdued. With my legs wrapped around it tightly, I towed my way along the muddy bottom toward the bank. As the water shallowed I easily got another breath and heaved the croc toward the bank. Once on dry land I lay on top of the croc to recuperate. Easily dragging the tired croc to my 4WD, I was able to strip off my seat cover with my teeth, then wrap it around his eyes as a blindfold. Now the pain in my fingers was starting to set in. I positioned the gorgeous little croc between my knees and released my grip on its head. It responded by releasing my fingers. Thank goodness.

Within a few minutes I'd managed to place the croc into a hessian bag, tie it up, and lock it in the front of my 4WD. My fingers and hand went numb and I was starting to feel a sharp pain under my eye.

It's important to cover the croc's eyes quickly to minimize stress.

Now, where's my boat? I thought. I couldn't hear the outboard so I shouted to my girl, "Chilli! Chilli, where are you, mate?"

Nothing, not a sound.

"Chilli, Chilli, cooee! Chilli girl—where are ya, Chill?"

Whoof, she barked in response.

Oh, no, she was upstream in the flow of the tide. Without a thought for safety or my injuries, I dived straight back into the dark, murky water and swam in her direction. When I reached the boat Chilli started licking my face so affectionately I couldn't swing up into the boat.

"Yes, I love *you,* my girl, but let me in!" I ordered.

Lick, lick, lick, she continued. I pushed her aside, flung myself in, fired up the outboard, and headed back to the boat ramp, eager to secure my catch and tend my wounds.

Once the croc was snug and secure in a wooden crate, I turned on the interior light to check out my bites and hits.

"Yep, your fingers are gonna need stitching, Stevo," I muttered to myself.

When I looked into the rearview mirror I was a little startled to see a huge open gash stemming from the corner of my eye along my cheekbone. "There goes my chances at television!"

I guess I must've been still pumped with adrenaline because instead of going straight to Townsville hospital I wrapped a rag around my fingers, dropped the small croc off at N.P.W.S. headquarters, and went back to my camp. Skilled at administering my own first aid, I soaked my wounds in antiseptic, took a couple of aspirins, and fell asleep in my swag all curled up with my girl, Chilli.

Blue-winged kookaburras sounded the familiar wake-up call. *Kook! Kook! Kook! Ka! Ka! Ka!*

Waking with a start, I muttered, "The traps! Gotta check the traps!" As I tried to get up, a sharp stab of pain near my eye made me wince. The pillow was stuck to my wound, which had been oozing all night. In a fit of aggression I ripped the pillow away from my face, pulling the wound open.

"Damn it!" I swore.

Trapping crocs on Cattle Creek.

"Damn! My hand is sore," I swore again.

This was no place to get a raging infection and I thought it better to soak my wounds and patch them up before I checked the traps. Tedious and time-consuming as it was, I took the time to dress my wounds properly. The whole time I was swearing and cursing as I knew the tide was coming in and the sun would be up in minutes.

Happy with my first aid, I wasted no time getting my boat in the water and speeding off to check the traps. As I sped around the S-bend I could see the trap site but no lead-in bait.

Excellent. Last night the croc had taken the lead-in, so things were looking good for a capture. Once a croc takes a lead-in, it's only a matter of time before it will enter the trap for the big piece of bait.

Over the next five nights, this crocodile ate the lead-in baits every night. On the sixth night I decided to leave a huge piece of fresh meat in the trap, with no more lead-ins.

The next morning, just on daylight as I rounded the S-bend and spotted the trap site, I noticed the weight bag had dropped. The trap had gone off! A little puzzled as to what had happened, I slowly headed toward the trap. It was totally submerged beneath the muddy, tea-colored water on a full moon high tide.

"What the hell's going on here?" I asked Chilli.

She just stared at me, loving the attention.

Thinking to myself that I'd have to come back at low tide to reset the trap, I cut the outboard and began to lean over and feel for the trap mesh. As I did, a jet of water spat up at me like a whale's blowhole.

"Holy heck! I've got one!"

The water erupted into a whirlpool of murk and turbulence. Think quick, Stevo, what are ya gonna do?

With both croc and trap totally invisible beneath the water, I strained my brain for a decisive approach.

Tenderly I felt for the mesh of the trap with an oar. Gently I eased some mesh to the surface, then grabbed it with both hands. I was easily able to secure some mesh around the bow hook, as if there was nothing in the trap.

Then all hell broke loose.

The trapped croc plowed its head into my boat with such force it knocked me back to the floor with my dog. Back on my knees I shouted at Chilli to stay down.

Quiet again, I grabbed more mesh and hooked it over the bow. Again there was an almighty thump as the angry croc took to my boat.

I gained some more mesh. Before long the huge triangular scoots of the croc's tail were visible. I hooked more mesh. As I grabbed for even more, the croc launched up out of the water and smashed its head and teeth into my boat. Chilli was shaking uncontrollably.

"Stay down, sweetheart, stay down," I commanded.

With an almighty heave I now had the croc's tail over the bow. This really made him angry and in a massive lunge the crocodile, pivoting off its tail, launched straight at me. I grabbed

Chilli under my arm and jumped into the water as the ballistic croc attacked with such force, he landed straight in the boat.

"Holy snappin' duck poo!" I gurgled in the armpit-high water.

Chilli quickly swam to the mangroves as I sliced at the ropes from the weight bag. *Bang!* The croc drove its gnarled, steel-like head into the side of the boat, denting it like a Coke can.

Throwing the ropes over the entangled croc and boat, I sucked in a breath and dived under the boat. Within seconds I threw the rope over again and again, each time diving under the boat to entwine the croc and boat completely with ropes. Not happy with that, I drew my knife and hacked off big, bushy mangrove branches and threw them on top of the now almost-

Trapping crocs Irwin-style: It can be muddy work.

subdued crocodile. Gingerly, I leaned over the bow and pulled out some hessian bags, which I accurately tossed on top of the croc's head as a temporary blindfold. His huge teeth bit deep into the bags in response. Perfect, I thought, he's almost blindfolded himself.

Without wasting a second, I pulled the boat up to the mangroves, threw in a reluctant Chilli, and fired up the outboard. The start of the outboard really annoyed the croc and he bit down on the bags in retaliation.

With the combined weight of the croc, Chilli, and myself, and the water we'd taken in, the small twelve-foot boat was on the verge of sinking. As I gunned it toward camp, the croc's head butted the boat so ferociously it split the aluminium. Water started squirting in. I thrust the boat into full throttle and headed straight for the mangroves. *Whoosh!* We pierced through the foliage and beached on the muddy bank. With desperation setting in, I bailed some water then jammed the boat into reverse. Once free from the mud, I again gunned it toward camp.

On the way back to camp the croc thrashed and tried to death roll. We took in more water and were forced to beach ourselves again. Again I bailed out water then took off. Then we were at the boat ramp where I slammed into the bank, ran a rope from my 4WD to the boat, engaged low, and dragged both croc and boat across the salt pans and mudflats back to my camp.

Confident now that I was on dry land, I positioned the truck's bullbar against the side of the boat and tipped the boat over until the croc rolled out and onto the ground.

Now I felt sorry for the croc. On dry land, thinking I was going to kill him, the poor old croc's eyes were wide open. I realized I had to move fast. If I didn't get this bloke boxed up and blindfolded, stress would get the better of him.

Desperately, I fought the cramps in my forearms to secure a top-jaw rope. Then another and another. With three top-jaw ropes secured, I rapidly unraveled the mesh of the trap. Exhausted and in fear, the croc fought with the little energy it still had. Then it succumbed to the strength of the ropes as I dragged a wooden crate toward its head. As if it were planned, Chilli nipped the croc's tail, which caused him to walk straight into the box.

"Wow, too easy." I spoke too soon. The powerful head of the croc smashed into the end of the box and split it wide open. With a reflex action I dragged another bigger box in front of the croc. As he smashed through one box he virtually had nowhere to go but up into the bigger box. I curled up his tail and pushed with all my weight. Obligingly, the croc lurched forward, allowing me to slam shut the end.

"Gotcha!"

Agro by name and by nature. To this day, this particular crocodile commands a lot of respect. He's never forgiven me for catching him and every day at home in the park he tries relentlessly to even the score. I have the utmost respect for him as he's nearly got me on numerous occasions. He's killed two lawnmowers, a brush hook, a shovel, my shoe, and my hat in his quest to remove me from his territory. I understand his territorialism and try hard not to upset him, but if he sees, hears, or smells me he'll submerge and poise for an ambush.

Gotcha! Chilli helps me to sort out crating this big croc.

Our daily croc demonstrations are the highlight of his day. He enjoys the opportunity to show off to his beautiful female companions Cookie and Mary. When the demos start he looks to his girls as if to say, "Watch me, girls, I'll protect you." Then he strikes with lightning speed straight toward me. His crocodilian ambush techniques and lightning-fast strikes are the perfect way to show park patrons exactly how a croc attack occurs. This makes it easy to educate people about the dangers of the often unseen predator. Which in turn is helping crocodile conservation.

Agro has never forgiven me for catching him and he tries to make a meal of me whenever he can.

Chapter V

To the Top

Far North Queensland contains patches of lush tropical rainforest that teems with bio-diversity. These steamy jungles are among the lushest places on earth, with some rainforests containing more species of flora and fauna than the whole of some countries. My interest, or should I say passion, for the tropical rainforests of Cape York Peninsula was kindled when I was a boy traveling with my parents on field trips.

On one such trip I was darting through the dense undergrowth looking for lizards with Dad and Mum. Spotting a dragon on a huge mossy granite boulder in the creek below, I shouted to Mum, "I'm gonna catch that one," and proceeded to run down the steep rocky bank toward the creek. *Whammo!*

My neck nearly snapped as it was thrown backward and my body was jerked off the ground. This was my first experience with the "wait a while" vine. I'd run straight into its long barbs, which had driven deep into my face and stopped me in my tracks. One of nature's traps.

I screamed to Mum for help and she was quickly with me and pulled down on the spring-loaded vine until dozens of barbs came free from the skin of my face. Off I went again, wiping the blood off as it oozed from my cheek, chin, and ear. It wasn't long before I spotted another lizard, then another. A couple of hours swept by and I could hear Dad calling me from up the gully. As I scampered up to him he asked me if I'd seen my mother. I hadn't.

"You head up the gully then back to the truck and I'll see if I can find her," Dad commanded.

As a young bloke I had exceptional direction and orienteering skills, which led me back to our truck with ease, effortlessly negotiating the mountainous gorges and incredibly dense foliage that engulfed our truck. Within moments I got bored so I started to dig worms and toss them into the crystal clear creek where the hungry jungle perch would snatch them up. Every now and then I'd try and trick them by tossing in a twig rather than a worm. They would rush it thinking it was more food and then back off, realizing it was inedible.

Trips with my parents to the steamy rainforest of far North Queensland were the start of a love affair with this area.

Hearing a loud rustling coming from a thick patch of rainforest, I yelled out, "Dad! Dad! Did you find her?" There was absolutely no reply and the noise of leaves being crushed underfoot was now coming closer. Feeling very vulnerable and alone I sat motionless on the large mossy boulder.

A cassowary! Remember, Stevo, stay very quiet and still or it may attack, I thought. The giant bird walked straight out of the thick scrub into the clearing and looked straight at me. I was trying really hard to be a part of this rock but the bird kept coming straight to me. It stopped only feet away and looked right at me. It twisted its head from side to side as if confused.

A little tearful, I said to the immense blue-headed bird, "Have you seen my mum?"

The tropical forest teems with wildlife including cassowaries.

No sooner had I got the words out than its eyes went wide and its head shot forward. Then it jumped and kicked the air and took off like a goanna in the midday sun. It tucked its helmeted head down and vanished through the thickest patch of "wait a while" vine. The helmeted head and coarse plumage of the cassowary allows it to glide through thick, impenetrable scrub with ease.

A long time passed and I was getting really worried about Mum, who was obviously lost. My faith in Dad's extraordinary bush skills was the only thing holding back the panic and tears. As I leaned back on the tires of his truck, the pristine beauty of the rainforest tantalized my senses; unusual, breathtakingly beautiful birds of various species singing, and the crisp clear smell of the deep dark forest. I wasn't game to leave the truck and search for lizards or my mum—I knew I had a job to do and that was to stay where I was.

Finally, after a very long time, I saw Mum and Dad winding their way up the overgrown track toward me. I was embarrassed at the tears rolling down my cheeks and desperately tried to dry them up so Dad didn't think I was a sook. But, by crikey, I love my mum! As I pulled away from her embrace I could see her face. She was exhausted and flustered.

It was during these hours alone in the rainforest that I dreamed of becoming a zoologist who would one day be able to cite the scientific names of every rainforest species.

At seventeen years of age I got my driver's license. I saved money religiously so that I could buy a car, and at eighteen I bought the first of my four-wheel drives. It was a clapped-out old yellow Toyota Hilux that had more rust than metal. I stripped it down to the chassis then spent many months restoring it to a good working truck that I knew back to front. This now yellow-and-black Hilux 4WD was to turn people's heads from one end of the country to the other. And "Old Yella," as I called it, was to be my home for nearly two months during a research trip to the Cape York Peninsula.

In 1985 the first specimens of an undescribed species of goanna were shot dead out of the rainforest canopy on the Peninsula. These specimens were collected for the Queensland Museum and used there to describe this new species.

From the moment I heard and read about this new goanna I felt compelled to help the species by studying live specimens. Dad was very supportive and he helped me to plan a seven-week trip up to the Cape to study both the goanna and green pythons.

It was to be the trip of a lifetime. I lived out of "Old Yella" totally entrenched in the jungle. Living like a possum, I'd occasionally come down out of the trees for a feed. Fortunately, God blessed me with orangutan arms. To study arboreal animals you've got to become one: I could climb anything.

I was so disappointed when it was time to go home to the Park but I'd gained a wealth of rainforest experience. Dad and Mum were envious and delighted with my knowledge on the new goanna species, and Dad and I decided that the next step in our research was to collect a pair of these goannas and study their breeding and behavior patterns.

Green python. What a little steamer!

Easily the toughest task was going to be catching these rare, elusive reptiles as they ran through the canopy like I run on a footy field. The museum people had had to shoot the goannas out of the canopy to catch them. I would have to catch them by hand with the least amount of stress and disturbance. I just love a mission.

It certainly turned out to be a lengthy mission. Dad was granted a permit to collect the goanna, then known as *Varanus prasinus,* in 1988 but it wasn't until 1992, after years of painstaking tree climbing, that we'd gained enough knowledge to observe them easily and capture them. Our years of research and study has revealed much needed data on the species and I've now published several scientific manuscripts. Now known as *Varanus keithhornei,* the species has a descriptive common name as well—I've called them "canopy goannas."

Mate! Can I climb trees!

It was November 1993 that Dad, Mum, myself, Terri, and my gorgeous dog Sui went into the thickest jungle in Cape York Peninsula to try and capture two pairs of canopy goannas.

A canopy goanna found curled up inside a hollow branch.

Mate! Can I climb trees! We spotted our first goanna scratching through the leaf litter for insects to eat. Once it heard us coming, it bolted straight up a huge tree. Without even thinking, I scrambled straight up the tree after it. Dad, Mum, and Terri surrounded the bottom of the tree and watched it closely to tell me where it was. It jumped from tree to tree—so did I. We were forty to fifty feet up and cutting across the thin branches of the canopy. Dad's eyes were deadly—he watched the goanna go into a long, thin tree. I took the leap of my life and grabbed on—but missed the goanna. It flew up a thin, thin branch, but I managed to dislodge it, and as it hesitated to get a better grip, I made a grab and got it. Yes! I shimmied down the tree so fast my ears popped.

We were all so excited—the start of a breeding program of a goanna species so rare it was brand new to science. We ended up catching two pair of canopy goannas in less than a week. Several months later, we bred the goannas in our specially designed Canopy Goanna Breeding Facility. All the eggs hatched perfectly and I've got to say that baby canopy goannas are absolutely darling. After we bred both pairs and established much needed scientific data and manuscripts, we took them back to Cape York Peninsula where they came from and let the whole lot go: adults, babies, and all.

That's what we're all about at Australia Zoo—securing information

Loaded up, heading on another mission.

so that in the event a species like the canopy goanna becomes endangered, we have the published information to ensure we can easily and effectively breed the animals so that we can release them back into the wild.

Canopy goannas are not very cuddly, but by crikey, they need our love. Like all of our wildlife, we have to understand them to conserve them. Our scientific research in the jungles of North Queensland is often hot and sweaty but always rewarding. The notorious taipan is one of the species I respect most. We encounter them often yet always unexpectedly. They are considered the most dangerous animal in our tropical North and should be avoided at any cost. It's important that we have a complete understanding and respect for the taipan. Without this apex predator the tropical North's biological diversity will diminish.

Canopy goanna. What a little beauty!

Chapter VI

The American Invasion

My first trip to Australia happened because of a chance meeting with an old school friend while I was celebrating my twenty-second birthday. I'd known John since kindergarten. We'd grown up together and he seemed more like family than a friend.

When he told me that he was leaving to spend a year in Australia, I was green with envy. He suggested that I should go over for a visit, too, and that started me seriously thinking about it. A trip that far away sounded both fantastic and frightening. This first Australian adventure took me from Manly, New South Wales, all the way to the Great Keppel Islands in Queensland. I was pleasantly surprised to discover that I actually had feelings of homesickness leaving Australia. I'd fallen in love with this country of sunshine.

My next visit didn't happen until several years later. It was the summer of 1991 when a friend of mine, Lori, invited me to accompany her on a diving trip to Australia. At this point in my life I was quite settled in Oregon and flying off to Australia wouldn't be easy. I was paying off a house, running the family business and a wildlife rehabilitation facility, and working part-time at an emergency veterinary hospital. I didn't even have time for a social life, much less to fly halfway around the world. However, I had begun to live by the philosophy of grabbing hold of opportunities whenever life offers them: when opportunity knocks, break down the door! So I rounded up the money, called Lori, and September 1991 saw us arriving in Brisbane.

Lori had arranged for us to stay with two of her friends and we spent several days shopping, enjoying the nightlife, and relaxing in the sun. The only things missing were the things Lori and I found the most interesting. Lori hadn't yet gone diving and I hadn't yet visited a single zoological facility. On our last weekend in Australia we agreed to take that diving trip. I was going to go along and enjoy the boat ride as diving has always been a little too scary for me.

Before diving that weekend we headed for the Sunshine Coast and a good old Aussie barbecue. I couldn't know that this day would change my life forever.

On the way to the barbecue we drove all the way up to Noosa, enjoying the sights along the way. On the way back, we turned off onto the Glass House Mountains Road. It was mid-afternoon and I was a bit sleepy after a late Saturday night out on the town, so I started dozing off in the back seat. I woke to find that we had turned off the main road. As I looked around to see where we were

The Glasshouse Mountains, location of the Reptile and Fauna Park.

Steve in the early nineties.

I saw a sign that read "Queensland Reptile and Fauna Park." I figured it must be just a little roadside zoo with a few snakes in a shed, but desperately needing a wildlife "fix," I decided to head in.

As we went in, we were informed that there was a crocodile demonstration going on and we hurried over to the demonstration area. As I maneuvered my way to the center of the crowd I saw two men with a large crocodile talking about the reptile's eating habits and territorial behavior.

Before I really knew what was happening, one of the men calmly walked up to the croc and held out a piece of food. As the croc's huge head lifted up and his powerful jaws opened wide, it astounded me how cool and collected this zookeeper seemed. I was used to the hype and fanfare that went with even the simplest task when handlers were working with dangerous wild animals in the United States, and here was an Aussie bloke with one of the most dangerous animals on earth looking more like he was mailing a letter than depositing food into bone-crushing jaws. What's more, he spoke with genuine love and affection about a crocodile that was large enough to consider the keeper himself as a food item.

I was captivated. Sadly, the demonstration was quickly over. A million questions went through my mind and I desperately wanted to see more. Then we were told that another crocodile demonstration would start in just a few minutes in the environmental park. I couldn't get to the admissions office fast enough to buy my ticket. What luck!

The keeper I'd seen was back for this demonstration as well. His enthusiastic love for these animals was contagious. It became impossible to see freshwater crocodiles as snappy little monsters. As he continued his talk I found my focus shifting from these most impressive crocodiles to the man who was speaking so passionately about them.

When we came to the last enclosure, the keeper began explaining why and how the crocodiles are caught out of the bush. I didn't need to be convinced that someone could be frightened of even a small crocodile; that was easy to believe. The amazing part was the way the crocodiles were captured. The keeper told of going out at night in a small boat and locating the crocs by their eyes glowing red in the glare of a spotlight. As one man idled the boat up to the crocodile, another keeper would position himself at the bow of the boat. As soon as the boat was close enough, he would leap into the water and grab the croc around the neck. As the crocodile struggled, man and beast would end up at the bottom of the river. After a bounce off the bottom, the crocodile would be flipped into the boat and become the driver's problem from there!

This was too incredible. Who was this man who spoke so casually of jumping into the water to wrestle crocodiles? He looked to be about my age and wasn't wearing a wedding ring, but surely this wonderful guy must have already been snapped up by some lucky girl. How could I possibly get a chance to talk to him, anyway?

As we were leaving this enclosure for our final educational talk in the museum area, I was struggling to think of something terribly witty to say. I had no idea of how to get the keeper's attention when I turned around to see Lori talking to him. I couldn't believe it! I edged my way out of the crowd and waited for Lori to catch up. As I looked toward them, his eyes met mine. It was as if we had always known each other. As I edged closer, he smiled and introduced himself as Steve Irwin.

We started talking and became lost in conversation. Maybe a few minutes went by, or maybe an hour. All I knew was that I wanted this day to go on forever. Suddenly, we were aware of a car horn blaring in the car park. I had to go. As we walked toward the entrance I realized that I didn't even know if Steve was "taken" or not! He seemed to realize what I was thinking

I was relieved to discover that Sui was not a human competitor for Steve's affections.

as he smiled and asked me if I'd like to meet his girlfriend. Had I misunderstood the chemistry between us? How could I feel such a strong attraction with someone who already had a girl?

Steve was calling out to Sui now, so I tried not to look the way I felt. Inside I was dying. As he continued to call out, a little brindle dog came running up. I was then formally introduced to his girlfriend, Sui. Steve said that Sui was his little Staffordshire bull scrub yowie and he loved her dearly. This only made Steve even more special to me and I wondered how I'd ever get to see him again.

I was about to leave the park and walk out of Steve's life forever when he handed me a park brochure with his name hastily written on it. He told me that he hoped he would see me again.

I must admit that the barbecue that afternoon was just a blur. My wheels were turning, trying to figure out a way to see this man again. Lori and I boarded a bus for Byron Bay and all I could do was think about Steve. When we returned to Brisbane I'd made my decision. I called Steve to ask if I could come visit the park again while Lori was spending the day scuba diving. Not only did Steve think this was a good idea, he invited me to stay at the park for the entire weekend. I agreed in an instant. Since Steve's parents and sister also lived at the park, I decided not to worry.

I was terribly nervous as Lori and her friends drove me up to the park on Friday afternoon. Lori and Julie were teasing me about my handsome crocodile-wrestler and my heart was pounding so hard I was sure it could be heard.

Steve took me to the house, and there I met his sister Mandy, and his mum, Lyn, and his dad, Bob. Bob, Steve, and I sat on the sofa and discussed the work I was doing in the United States with predatory mammals. I think my cougar rescue work interested them as much as their crocodile rescue work interested me.

Steve had arranged for me to stay at the Glasshouse Mountains Motel and when we arrived to check in, the couple who operate the motel were having a bit of a giggle at Steve's expense. They merrily announced that they'd given me the honeymoon suite!

Steve and I were to have dinner at Caloundra and the drive there went by all too quickly. I don't remember the road at all. I only had eyes for Steve as he told story after story of his bush adventures.

When we went in to eat I was pleased to discover it was a seafood buffet. We grabbed our plates and merrily piled them high with mud crab. While we were eating and talking, Steve suddenly got a very misty look in his eyes and I steadied myself for his saying something terribly romantic. Instead,

Steve and me in Los Angeles in 1995.

with awe in his voice, he looked down at the crab spread up to my elbows and said, "Gosh, you're not ladylike at all!" Lucky for me, this was a good thing.

When Steve dropped me back at the motel there was no tension over that first kiss. There was no first kiss at all! I had prepared myself the entire drive back for the possibility and, instead, Steve simply said that he'd be back first thing in the morning.

He was back, first thing, as promised. As I scrambled to get my things together and get out the door, I wondered what the day would hold. It was turning out to be a typical hot Queensland day. When we arrived at the park, Steve handed me a rake and it was suddenly down to business. I was painfully aware of my sweat-drenched hair and flushed face when we'd finished raking the park clean of leaves and debris. Steve didn't seem even to notice as we sat down for the mid-morning "smoko" break. And it amazed me to see Bob and Steve sit down to a hot cup of tea when all I wanted was a cold glass of water.

After our break Steve decided to show me something of the community he lived in. We visited the local museum, oceanarium, rainforest, and finally the Glasshouse Mountains lookout. The view was breathtaking and we were all on our own. Once again my heart began to pound. Surely this would be an appropriate spot for our first kiss? But instead, Steve proudly told me the names of all the surrounding mountains and landmarks before starting up the truck to go. Strike two!

The following morning Steve arrived late to pick me up. Although he had just been getting some work done at the park and letting me sleep in, I was sure that he was losing interest in me. But, later, as Steve drove me back to Brisbane for my last night in Australia, I had to admit this was something much more than a chance meeting. It felt like fate.

As the plane left the ground departing for the U.S., I reflected on the past week and wondered what would happen next. And, yes, I got my kiss!

It was a cold autumn night not long after I returned to Oregon that I got a call from that familiar Aussie voice. Steve and I talked a bit, catching up with how all of our animals were doing, as well as how much we missed each other. Then he totally surprised me by announcing that he would be coming over for a ten-day visit in a month's time. I couldn't believe it! I immediately made arrangements to take time off work and started counting the days until he arrived.

The day before Steve's arrival I finalized my welcoming plans. I bought a new dress and rented a limousine to pick him up from the airport. A dear friend of mine, Cathy, even helped me get my house together so everything was perfect for Steve's arrival. Everything was perfect,

Steve's trip to Oregon allowed him to enjoy a variety of wildlife very different to his beloved Australian creatures.

all right, except Steve. He wasn't feeling well, poor guy. While I was excited to show him the town, he just wanted a rest!

The next day Steve was feeling his old self again and we loaded the car to take off and see Oregon. Now it was my turn to show Steve around. As we headed east through the Cascade Mountains, Steve was thrilled to get to stop and explore a beaver dam. Squirrels and raccoons were a new thrill, too. The wildlife in the Pacific Northwest is radically different from the wildlife Down Under.

We spent a magical ten days together and, once again, it was painful to part. I promised Steve that I would come over for another visit as soon as I had the money. Meanwhile, Telecom profited highly, as we spoke by phone nearly every day.

Steve's visit had been in November. Now it was January 1992 and I was landing in Brisbane again.

I stayed with Steve's family at the park for four weeks. Most of the time I was there we worked together. Since I wanted to help clean enclosures Steve said that I would have to be properly introduced to a baby crocodile! Steve gently picked up a

Raccoons were a new thrill for Steve.

A neonate crocodile.

neonate croc, held it out to me, and with a smile told me to let it bite me. At first I thought I must have misunderstood. I mean, sure, this croc was only about seven inches long, but wouldn't it hurt? Steve patiently explained that I needed to learn not to jerk my hand away if I was bitten because I could severely damage the little croc. I could see his point. I didn't want to fling one halfway across the room if it latched hold of me! I gritted my teeth and held out my hand. I felt a little pinch, but this tiny croc could barely even break the skin.

After spending time acquainting myself with the park's inhabitants (both staff and animals), Steve announced that we would be going bush. I was terribly excited and a little bit nervous at the thought. Steve packed the truck and we headed north. Steve wanted to survey the crocodiles in a river system that represented their southernmost stronghold. Of course, we took along little Sui. It was her job to sit in the truck and jealously glare at me!

Upon reaching the river, we had about an hour and a half of four-wheel driving to reach Steve's favorite campsite. With the road washed out into gullies in some places and the boat making us extremely top-heavy, the drive was treacherous at times.

We arrived in time to set up camp before the sun went down. Beautiful boulders spread out into the river before me, worn smooth over the years during times of flood. Steve selected this spot years ago when he first came here to catch problem crocs. Since then he'd been coming here regularly. He knew this river like the back of his hand.

When it got dark, Steve got the boat ready to go out and spot crocodiles. Since crocs are primarily nocturnal, nighttime on the water is both the best time and most dangerous time to spot them. Steve packed two spotlights and batteries along with our other gear. He showed me how best to see the crocodiles' eyeshine by holding the spotlight right under my nose. The night was very dark and the overhanging trees looked eerie as we dimmed our spotlights to scan for the glowing red eyes of the crocodiles. As we traveled upriver, the insects were attracted to the spotlights by the thousands. I felt them in my hair, down my shirt, and fluttering all over my face, yet I barely noticed them for the splashing by our boat. Every now and then something would splash like it was up having a look at us and then would make a hasty retreat. Steve seemed to sense that I was uneasy. He explained that the river was full of tortoises, fish, and frogs and that we weren't close to any crocodiles yet.

As we continued upriver, Steve started spotting crocodiles. Over the next two or three hours, Steve pointed out several. Most were small—six to eight feet in length—and quite shy. But the last one we saw, the furthest up the river, was enormous. It would definitely have been over ten feet in length and, try as we might, we could only pick up the eyeshine of one of its eyes. After pursuing it for several minutes, we decided it must have been injured—possibly shot. It was marvelously elusive, though, so it could have been an old injury.

As Steve turned the boat to return to camp he had his hands full. He was trying to maneuver the boat, spotlight the crocodile, and answer my millionth whispered question. As a result, the boat became lodged in a huge patch of weeds. Steve instructed me to conserve our battery

Me and Sui looking for crocs.

Steve and me rafting.

power. In a blink we were left with no moonlight, no spotlight—only complete darkness. While Steve negotiated the boat, I looked up at the billions of winking stars until my eyes adjusted. My senses seemed to sharpen. The river was alive with movement and I became aware of every little action around me, even as the hairs stood up on the back of my neck! As the fruit bats flapped noisily above, I don't think I'd ever felt so alive.

Steve soon dislodged the boat and we were on our way again. I put aside my fantasies of monstrous crocodiles stalking us from every side and concentrated on the beauty of this nighttime world. We floated along in total darkness for a while until Steve needed the spotlight again to light the way. For the first time I noticed the tiny bats flitting right in front of my nose catching the insects attracted to the light. As we approached camp I wished this night would never end. And I felt I understood the passion that drove Steve to protect such river systems and the crocodiles that lived in them. I'd endured too much adrenaline for one day. I tried to stay awake and watch the stars, but obviously didn't manage to because the next thing I knew, it was morning.

Steve cooked a beautiful breakfast over the fire and we discussed our plans for the day. Sui loved nothing more than helping Steve search for pigs to check out their growing numbers in the area, and also survey the damage they were doing to the environment. As it was getting late in the morning, the day was really warming up. Steve said that it was far too hot for pigs to be out and about, but Sui should be able to flush them out of the rubber vine. This vine, like the pigs, has taken over in some areas of the country. It's extremely dangerous for a dog to enter it with a pig as the vine is far too dense for a dog to maneuver through. However, it's perfect for the pigs. They move through these chokingly thick bushes with apparent ease. In a large patch of rubber vine, humans are at risk as well.

We took the boat across the river and began our search for pigs on the other side. There was plenty of evidence from the multitude of tracks that we were in an area that had been frequented by pigs only days ago. It was Sui that picked up the fresh tracks. She began yelping in earnest, as if telling Steve to hurry up. Steve disappeared ahead of me and I could hear him crashing through the bush, catching up with his dog. I ran as fast as I could through the pressing heat.

I started to feel as if my chest was being constricted; it was hard to get air and I wasn't sure how much farther I could go on when I heard Steve yell something from up ahead. I couldn't hear what he said, so I ran a little further and stopped to call out to him. Steve was yelling at me to continue to call out my location. He and Sui were right on the pigs now and he didn't want me to get caught by them running back my way. This made me run all the harder. I figured it would be a really good idea if Steve could see me as well as hear me!

All at once I broke into a small clearing and the thick vine around me was alive with motion. Pigs started bursting out of the vine and charged right past me. I yelled out to Steve. He was close, just on the other side of a large section of vine, and he told me to look for a sturdy tree. I heard the urgency in his voice and looked around to see nothing but vine. I started to run, but more pigs came rushing out of the vine so I stood perfectly still, frozen like a statue.

As suddenly as the frenzy started, it stopped. Not a sound could be heard, just my own breathing. I called out to Steve, but he was already on his way over to me. After a brief discussion to check that we were both OK, it suddenly occurred to both of us at the same time that Sui's barking had stopped. We had a quick look around and called out to her, but still there was nothing.

We decided to split up and parallel each other up the river. We ran about a half mile and then started seeing huge pig tracks along with Sui's tracks. Sometimes Sui's paw prints disappeared and there was evidence that she had struggled with the pig and had been dragged along through the mud. Suddenly Steve came upon Sui and the pig. A huge boar was standing over Sui, preparing to finish her off. Sui was lying on her side, gasping for air and covered with mud. The moment this giant, snorting boar saw Steve it took off like a shot.

By the time I arrived, it was all over. Steve was kneeling over Sui, afraid to touch her. My first thought was that Sui must have been mortally wounded. She couldn't even raise her head. Steve knelt in the mud while I checked her from head to tail. Her gums were a muddy, pale color instead of nice and pink. All four legs were limp and she showed no response when I pinched her toes. Externally, she was showing very little evidence of damage. But what was going on internally? I was certain that she was terribly wounded: I was afraid to tell Steve, but I really thought she had a broken back. When Steve asked me what was wrong I told him that I wasn't sure. We both agreed that we needed to get her back to camp.

When Steve arrived with the boat, Sui was still unable to move. Back at camp, Steve gently placed her on his swag and we discussed what to do next. I told Steve that I thought we should get her to a vet right away. Then Steve reminded me of our location. It would be at least an hour and a half of four-wheel driving to get out to the road. Instead Steve said that he'd bed down with her for the night and take it one step at a time.

We both stayed up late, watching Sui closely. Before I fell asleep I saw her raise her head. During the night Steve noticed her stir, trying to get comfortable. By morning she was able to

Steve, Sui, and me in the croc dinghy.

stand, although she was shaking badly. We took it easy all day and Sui slowly recovered. To this day, after discussing her condition with several veterinarians, her injuries and recovery remain a complete mystery.

When Sui felt up to it, we explored the river by day for signs of crocodiles. Our biggest find was an active crocodile nest site. Steve spotted the mound of leaves and debris raked into a giant nest about three feet tall and ten feet across. It was built on the high end of an island, as if the mother crocodile was trying to nest above flood level. Judging from the size of the nest, she must have been a large croc as well. I went up to the nest site with Steve to help document the find. The eggs were examined and carefully replaced. If Steve was excited by this find, I was overwhelmed! In all my life I never thought I'd get to experience something so special. We left as quietly as we came and rejoiced over the perfect eggs we had found.

That night Sui seemed to be back to her old self and we were still on a bit of a high from the day's find. I was feeling a bit dreamy, watching the stars, and I realized that I was really falling for Steve. It was definitely love. I was nearly asleep when I heard Steve's voice out of the darkness quietly asking me if it was still tradition to ask a girl's father first before proposing. I'm not sure what I said. My heart was pounding so hard I was sure Steve could hear it. I lay awake long into the night. I had a lot to think about.

We returned to the park later that week, safe and sound. There was no more talk of marriage, but a new feeling, almost electric, lingered between us. I was getting into the routine now. Everything from cleaning enclosures to crowd control and even serving in the shop was becoming easy now. But soon I'd be flying back to Oregon.

What with being with the staff all day and Steve's family all night there wasn't a lot of privacy, and we'd have to sneak off to some corner of the park to talk about the future and dream. One evening we sat under the fig tree next to the house and relaxed with a cool drink. We were discussing wildlife issues when Steve suddenly asked me to marry him. It wasn't as if I hadn't thought about this moment. I just never expected it so soon. Four months earlier Steve and I didn't even know each other. Then I heard a little voice say, "Yes, I will." The little voice was mine. It must have been! In the midst of this emotional moment, Steve's mum came out looking for us. She knew immediately what was going on and ran off to tell Steve's dad.

The next few days were a rush of celebration—telling the staff, parties, calling my parents, and trying to figure out a wedding date. We decided to marry in June. The wedding would be in my hometown in Oregon. Steve invited me to stay in Australia until the wedding, but I knew I had to get back. I would have less than four months to get ready to change my life forever.

Back in the States it was strange to be in the middle of winter again after leaving the subtropical Sunshine Coast. Time flew by as I made arrangements both to get married and to move so far away. Planning the wedding was a job of pure joy, but I became aware very quickly that some of this joy would be mixed with pain.

The first consideration was for my family. My parents had started their own business in the field of construction back in 1949. Growing up, I'd worked long hours learning this business from the ground up. Dad taught me how to type when I was just eight years old. And Mom was always coaching me on my printing and spelling skills. When I played with the other kids in the neighborhood I didn't play with dolls, I organized business enterprises selling products ranging from juice to old toys. (Of course, I was always the president of the "company.") It was only natural that after I got out of school, I would work full-time for my

Growing up in Oregon: I've always had an interest in the outdoors and in business!

parents. At twenty I was running the family business. Now one of my sisters was buying the business as I was severing my ties and moving on.

Next, I needed to sort out the other love of my life, "Cougar Country," a wildlife rehabilitation facility for predatory mammals. This, too, would have to be taken over by someone else and the responsibility for some three hundred animals a year (from bats to bobcats) would have to be passed on. The workload had proved to be too much for any of over

I didn't play with dolls, I organized business enterprises.

one hundred volunteers who worked with me. Finally, one woman agreed to follow through with my work, but only for the following twelve months. Seven years of wildlife rescue work in the Pacific Northwest would then also have to come to an end.

Most of the permanently held wildlife was eventually relocated to caring individuals who would look after them for the rest of the animals' lives. Some of these animals were too badly injured to be released back to the wild. That was the case with Chuck the raccoon. He had been terribly mauled by a dog when he was only about eight weeks old. His mother had been killed trying to defend her young from this marauding pet. Other animals were victims of the entertainment industry— like Malina the cougar. After performing in a movie, she found herself for sale in the exotic pet trade. Steve and I were hoping to get Malina to Australia, so I found her a temporary holding facility nearby.

Steve and I were hoping to bring Malina back to Australia.

Me and Malina, one of my cougar friends from "cougar country."

While I was in the States, Steve was facing the problem of moving Graham, one of the crocodiles. He had grown much more quickly than the other crocs in his enclosure and was fast becoming a danger to them. Steve was going to allow Channel 10 News to film the event, which would show the crocodile lured from the water with a food item so that Steve could drop a loop of rope over its top jaw. Then Steve would drag him from the water, jump on the croc's head, secure a blindfold, and move him . . . piece of cake!

Steve had trouble with Graham from the start. Channel 10 flew a film crew to the Park by helicopter—only to find Graham refusing to come out of the water. Several days later, a second attempt also failed. By the third attempt Steve was really feeling the pressure. He was determined to catch this croc for the camera.

As Graham showed interest in the food item, Steve stepped those few inches closer

The big day—we were married in Oregon.

to ensure the lasso would meet its mark. But at the last moment, Graham suddenly shifted his attention from the food item to Steve's hand holding the rope. In an instant, Graham had hold of Steve's right hand. As Graham began to drag Steve toward the water, Steve immediately moved with him to avoid losing his arm. When Graham pulled Steve into the water, Steve's only thought was of survival. Steve landed on Graham's head and instinctively tried to hang on. This two-hundred-pound weight was not exactly what Graham had anticipated and he let go to swim for deeper water.

Even as the staff were rushing to Steve's aid, it was all over. Channel 10 rushed to Brisbane with the footage and Steve was rushed to hospital. Graham's teeth had punctured holes completely through Steve's hand. Steve carefully explained to me that night that he'd made a mistake but this wasn't an easy situation for me to handle. It was a mistake that could have cost Steve his life. I felt a real sense of urgency to be with him again.

June was upon me almost before I realized it. Steve landed safely in Eugene, Oregon, with eight of his family and friends from Australia. We breezed through two days of rehearsals, dinners, and meeting with the minister. Then it was our wedding day.

The church was filled as nearly four hundred people came to wish us well. Even the minister seemed nervous as we stood ready to exchange our vows. When we were finally

proclaimed man and wife, a great calm came over me and I knew, beyond a shadow of a doubt, that I had made the right choice. I was joined with my soulmate for life.

The next day we prepared for our first adventure. After a whirlwind tour of Oregon, we headed back to Australia to begin filming our first wildlife documentary. A river system in North Queensland was the scene of an age-old conflict between humans and crocodiles. If we didn't get there quickly the situation could become critical—and it was the crocodiles that stood to lose.

Our proud parents at the wedding: my mom, Judy; Steve's dad, Bob; me and Steve; Steve's mom, Lyn, and my dad, Clarence.

Chapter VII

On the Road

Steve had been teaching me about crocodile behavior at the Park, but now I was about to embark on my first real experience with crocodiles in the bush. I was excited, but also a little nervous as we headed out.

We arrived at Camp Chilli in time to set up camp. There were six of us on this film shoot: the director, cameraman, soundman, Wes Mannion (Steve's best mate and one of our Park staff), and of course myself and Steve. We were well prepared for the tropical evening with a good supply of mosquito repellent. I have to admit that the mossies were most impressive: they positively seemed to drink the stuff. Not only did they seem immune to bug spray, they were able to bite through anything. Even the lawn chairs! And there were millions of them.

Through the night I listened to the sounds of koalas courting, fruit bats fighting, and herds of pigs moving around close to camp. Being a bit nervous about leaving the tent, I was eager to grab the dunny roll and find a nice, private bush first thing in the morning. I did not, however, expect to have to share my spot. Much to my shock I nearly stood on a huge, shiny snake. I must

have startled him as much as he scared me because he reared up, flattened his neck, and hissed. I lost all thoughts of having to relieve myself.

Steve came running when he heard me yelling for help and the cameraman was right on his heels. Having heard so many stories of Australia's taipan, I was sure that this was the snake I had disturbed. Steve assured me that it actually was a red-bellied black snake. Still quite venomous, but not as deadly as the taipan. So, dunny roll still in hand, I watched as Steve moved the huge snake safely away from our camp. It wasn't a terribly glamorous way to begin our filming, but it sure got my heart going! I also found it incredibly romantic to have my husband actually save my life on our honeymoon.

After recovering from that little heart starter, we got down to business. We had a job to do and that was locating and rescuing a large crocodile that was making local residents a bit nervous. We spent hours searching the river system for signs of the crocodile's presence. I was amazed to learn that, in spite of the wealth of wildlife living on the river, we'd have to film for hours on end just to get enough footage to edit down to a one-hour program.

The turning point on this trip came when we discovered that someone had beaten us to the big crocodile and had shot him dead. That evening we even discussed going home. But with other large crocodiles in the area, most of them female, we knew that they, too, would be in jeopardy. It became a race against time. We would have to try to relocate the dead crocodile's mate before the shooters got to her. Everyone's spirits lifted a bit as we tried to focus on our new goal instead of the tragedy we'd just witnessed.

The reality of the situation was that it could take weeks or even months to catch her. She would know what had happened to her mate and would now be more elusive than ever.

I was tired at the end of our first day of trying to locate her. We'd searched the river system for signs of her until the tide went out. Just on dark, still several hundreds of feet from camp, we literally ran out of water. We got out of the boat and proceeded to drag and float it the rest of the distance. Steve told me to hang on tight to the edge of the boat. Sometimes we would

Steve and Sui take a break from the outback heat.

walk right into a deep hole and abruptly sink in the chest-deep water. There was always a bit of a risk of landing on a crocodile!

By the time we made it back, I could barely climb the steep, muddy bank and weave my way through the mangroves to camp. The fireflies were just beginning to wink on and off as Steve and I joined the camera crew, falling in a heap around the fire. We looked a motley crew, thickly covered with mud from the knees down, but the lovely thing about the mud was that it helped to keep the swarms of mosquitos at bay.

It was now far too dark to risk going anywhere near the creek for a tub. As I was contemplating this, I noticed that things had gone quiet. I looked up at the crew and there were five pairs of eyes looking back at me. I knew I must look quite a sight, but I couldn't figure out why these five men just kept staring. Suddenly, the light dawned. Dinner! It was dinnertime and they were all looking at me!

I tried to quell the panic that was welling up inside. No one had mentioned that I'd be

cooking, too. It would have been awkward enough if I had been in a fully stocked kitchen—to this day I am not exactly hailed for my cooking ability—but cooking for six of us over an open fire was beyond my comprehension. This was definitely a tough moment, but after admitting my lack of experience, everyone pitched in and dinner was served. We ended up taking turns to wash up.

Later that night, after a luxurious bath in a bucket of cold salt water, Steve noticed a beautiful little ringtail possum. We decided to film the charming fellow and discovered that he had brought his family along, too. The mother possum was high up a nearby tree with her joey on her back. We set up lights to film them and got about three hours of them happily munching leaves. Steve was so impressed with how calm they were that he decided to climb the tree to try and get the camera a bit closer. This was our only option as the tree was very difficult to climb and Steve was the only one of us, besides the possums, who could do it.

When Steve got as close as he thought he should to the mother possum, he settled in on a larger branch and prepared to film. That's when I noticed something moving on him. I grabbed the binoculars for a better look and was

My introduction to the bush, Aussie-style.

Steve captures a juvenile saltwater crocodile in the mangroves.

horrified to see Steve teeming with ants. These ants weren't black, they were a light green color. And there were literally hundreds of them all over Steve's body. When I pointed out the obvious to Steve, he suggested that I examine some that were close to me on a tree limb. I scooped up a few which immediately decided that they didn't like being disturbed, and they began to bite my hands. It was a most incredible sensation. Almost like being stabbed with a hot needle! I began to do the green ant dance until I successfully shook every one off me. My entire green ant experience took only a few seconds, and yet Steve had been up in that tree with them for nearly an hour!

Steve had decided to show me a bit of bush tucker for breakfast, so you can imagine my dismay when he strolled into camp cradling a very large nest of green ants. Not again! But I must admit, I was most impressed when he stirred a few around in a glass of water. It tasted like lemonade. All I had to do was ignore the few hanging off my lips!

After a quick bite of breakfast, we prepared to head out on the river to continue searching for our female crocodile. The sun was barely up but we could all feel the heat. The flies began to buzz around in earnest now and I couldn't wait to escape them by zipping downstream in the boat. No sooner had we loaded the camera gear than we turned to find an unexpected visitor in camp. A lace monitor, attracted by our rubbish bin, had wandered in to look for food scraps. He was a delightful little fellow and looked so sweet as he flicked his forked tongue in and out, trying to pick up some scent particles that would lead him to a meal.

We decided to postpone our boat trip and film this little rascal instead. I was thrilled to get to pick him up and do a piece to the camera, explaining how special this lizard was. After all, none of Australia's lizards are venomous, so I felt quite safe. It was only after the "lacey" had finished exploring our camp and had wandered off that Steve bothered to mention that the lace monitor has teeth like a tiger shark. If even this small one had bitten me, it would have meant stitches.

Several days of searching passed before we finally found positive signs of our female crocodile. High up on the bank Steve spotted a mound of leaves. This was the nest site of our girl. She would have to be close, perhaps even watching us now. Near this location, at a likely sunning bank, Steve decided to set the trap.

The trap is made of sixteen-ton trawler mesh. It is designed to allow the crocodile easy access to a food item which, when grabbed, sets off a weight bag that falls from a tree, drawing the mouth of the trap shut. The trap is secured to a tree so that the crocodile can't walk off with it, and there they sit, caught in a giant sock, until we retrieve them. It sounds rather simple, but it took Steve and me the entire day to set it up.

Steve had told me there was no way our crocodile was just going to walk right in. We'd have to make her comfortable with this strange new thing in her environment. To do that, Steve would utilize a lead-in bait. The plan was to secure a fist-sized piece of meat on the end of a string and dangle it over the water. Gradually, the crocodile would become accustomed to these free handouts and would lose her fear of the presence of the trap.

First thing the next morning we headed out to bait up our crocodile trap. When we arrived at the site, there was very little sign of crocodile. The croc was still in the vicinity, but was probably being a bit cautious. Steve tied the piece of pork to a string. The string was then attached to a stick and the stick shoved in the mud, right in front of the trap. Now our lovely crocodile girl would get a free snack and maybe she would begin to lose her fear of the trap.

With the bait set, there was nothing to do but wait. Crocodiles are nocturnal so we wouldn't return to check on the lead-in bait until the following morning. Instead, we went with the film crew to explore more wildlife along the river.

Big Sky country: where to next?

As the day warmed up we began to keep an eye out for reptiles. Most people believe that reptiles are only seen on warm days because they are "cold blooded." Actually, their blood is not cold, but reptiles simply can't regulate their own body temperature as mammals can. In order to warm up, a reptile must get into the sun. If a reptile is too hot, it cannot sweat to cool down— it must get out of the sun or into the water. This makes it a very efficient animal. Some reptiles can go long periods without food because they do not rely on the energy from food to warm their bodies, as we mammals do.

Just before midday, Steve spotted a huge sand goanna foraging for food. We zoomed in to film him and he quickly abandoned his hunt for lunch and retreated underground. Steve scooped out this giant from his sandy hollow for the filming opportunity.

I really enjoyed meeting this giant lizard up close. He would have been nearly seven feet long and seemed to be as curious of me as I was of him. He had enormous forearms, reminding me of Popeye, and a long, forked tongue which he flicked out at me. Most lizards have a fat, fleshy tongue but goannas, or varanids, have a forked tongue like a snake's. And, just like a snake, they use their tongue to help pick up scent particles. As this enormous "sandy" lightly flicked his tongue over my face, he was actually smelling me. What an experience!

When we explored the area where the goanna had been searching for food, Steve uncovered a nest site just under the sand next to some rotting timber. The nest held ten or twelve little white eggs. I was stumped, but Steve knew immediately that they were lizard eggs. Upon closer inspection, we saw that some of the eggs were starting to hatch. I didn't fully appreciate at the time what an incredible find this was; I just figured Steve always came across lizard eggs from time to time. However, not since we filmed these precious little sand goannas have I witnessed goanna eggs hatching in the wild. Fortunately, the big male sand goanna, who might have made a meal of these hatchlings, was not sighted again.

In between all the goanna excitement, we would faithfully check the lead-in bait in front of our croc trap. Every morning we were disappointed; the piece of meat had not been touched. Steve was starting to lose patience. We were all too aware that this was a race against time. There was a crocodile poacher out there somewhere who was trying to catch this crocodile, too . . . but with a bullet. Steve began checking the lead-in bait earlier and earlier in the morning, even before it was light.

One morning, when we had all returned from checking the trap site, there were visitors waiting for us. I worried that something might be wrong. As we approached the campsite I could see an old battered Nissan tray-back with a cattle dog in the back. Two men had made themselves at home, each enjoying a cup of tea. The billy was still boiling as we greeted the two graziers.

The men turned out to be local farmers who'd heard through the bush telegraph that we were up catching crocodiles. As luck would have it, they had a crocodile problem of their own. Steve was all ears as we made ourselves comfortable around the fire to hear their story.

It appeared that several months earlier, this area had suffered an unusually rainy wet season. The "wet" in tropical North Queensland is always quite dramatic, but this season was phenomenal. The rain was so heavy and lasted so long that most of the area was under three feet of water. Cattle had to be moved to high ground near the homesteads and some

Crossing through floodwaters gives the crew the opportunity for some unusual filming.

Steve and Wes Mannion prepare to blindfold a croc to minimize stress.

folks were completely cut off from any form of transportation. Those in the area with mustering helicopters helped as best they could by dropping food and supplies to the stranded graziers.

The older of the two men continued to explain that it was when the water had receded that they discovered their predicament. Near the farmer's house was a small dam. As the floodwater disappeared, a young crocodile had taken refuge in this dam. It had been there several weeks, living miles from the river, before the farmer's wife saw it out sunning itself on the bank. Nobody believed the poor woman until it was spotted again. The younger of the two men piped up and claimed that he had seen the crocodile, too, and it must have been nearly ten feet long. The dam still held water, but would be completely dry by the end of the dry season.

We all agreed that something would have to be done. The crocodile would run out of water and die if it wasn't moved. I think our new friends would sleep better once it was gone, too! The crew was excited at the prospect of finally filming a crocodile capture, so we set out right away for the homestead.

When we arrived at the small dam, I was amazed that a crocodile of its size could be living there. It must have eaten any fish in the dam some time ago; surely, it was getting good and hungry by now. Steve asked to see exactly where the croc came out to sun itself and was directed to the general vicinity. Even though he assured the family that a crocodile this size was not big enough to hunt a person, no one else would go anywhere near the little pond!

Steve knelt down and surveyed the entire perimeter of the water. Although the area around the dam was mostly grassy, where the level of the water had dropped there was some exposed mud. Working like a detective, Steve finally found the faintest markings in the dried mud where a crocodile had dragged itself out of the water. Steve carefully analyzed the distance between the claw marks and decided that this crocodile was probably closer to seven feet long, not ten feet as earlier suggested. Steve smiled broadly and there was a mischievous glint in his eye. I knew he was up to something. By now the scorching afternoon sun was beating down, so we were only too happy to return to the homestead for a cool drink before discussing Steve's plan.

Steve was nearly bursting with excitement when he announced that we would simply net the crocodile out of the water, jump it, restrain and blindfold it, then return it to the river. A stunned silence filled the room. What seemed like a thrilling challenge to Steve struck the rest of us as a terrific risk. I asked Steve what our other options were and, although he looked terribly hurt that we didn't share his enthusiasm, he patiently explained why nothing else would work. My idea with the live trap would just take too long. And he couldn't jump on this crocodile from a boat because there was no room to maneuver the dinghy in the tiny dam.

Steve explained that if we approached the dam at night, I could back him up with the net while our Park manager, Wes Mannion, held the crocodile mesmerized in the beam of the spotlight. We were not convinced that using a net and approaching the situation at night was such a great idea, but we all trusted Steve's experience and skill.

We all had our jobs to do. The camera crew prepared tapes, lights, and extra batteries while Steve and I organized nets, ropes, and the all-important blindfold. We would wait until it was good and dark before going in. During daylight hours, a crocodile can remain submerged for over an hour at a time, surfacing underneath the camouflage of vegetation to take a breath, but in the dark the crocodile feels more secure. Our croc would surface then to have a look at us, and that would be the time to hit him with the spotlight. That was what we were waiting for. None of us could eat dinner that night. We were all nervous, waiting on edge for Steve to give the go-ahead to move in.

It was nearly 10 P.M. when Steve went out on his own, with his spotlight on dim, to scan the water. Steve nearly fell through the door after being away for only a few minutes.

Steve and I set up a trap.

"It's in the perfect spot!" he gushed. "What a little ripper!"

I felt the adrenaline surge through me as we all charged out to surround the dam. I sat breathless next to Steve as the dim spotlight swept over the water. The light came to rest on what appeared to be a small, red reflector in the water near the far bank. I felt Steve tense, then cautiously he turned the spotlight all the way up to dazzle the crocodile. In the same instant I was aware of Wes next to me, taking the light from Steve. It was time.

Steve went to the far end of the dam with what appeared to be a bait net. His plan was to encircle the crocodile with the fine mesh, allowing it to bite at the net. Once it was entangled in the mesh we would both pull the croc out of the water and jump on it . . . piece of cake!

Steve entered the water, dragging the net in with him. Cautiously he probed the murky water ahead of him with a stick. The last thing he wanted to do was accidentally stand on this already wary crocodile. As Steve went around the spotlight's beam, not only had the crocodile submerged back into the darkness of the water, but Steve began having some trouble with the net. It seemed to be tangled. I began to worry that this was taking too long. What if the crocodile panicked and attacked?

All I could do was hold my breath and watch. The spotlight never wavered as my eyes burned into the beam, desperately trying to locate any movement. Several minutes passed . . . it seemed like an eternity. Then, without any warning, the water began to churn and boil right next to the net. Steve began frantically shoving the net forward with his stick, trying to make the croc bite the net and get those sixty-four sharp teeth tangled in its mesh.

As abruptly as the struggle began, everything stopped, perfectly still. I could see the expression of frustration on Steve's face. This was taking longer than he expected, and every minute that went by made the crocodile more nervous and the situation more treacherous. Steve couldn't afford to wait for the crocodile's next move. He began easing forward, pushing the net ahead of him through the water. Ever aware of the presence of the camera, Steve also tried to explain what was going on out of sight under the water.

As Steve would take a step forward, the crocodile would try to escape past him, only to be stopped by the net. The crocodile's body whipped at Steve as it tried to dart past his legs. When the croc was close enough, Steve would try to jam some of the net in its mouth with his stick, only to feel the crocodile's head slam into his legs as it tried to escape. Every time the crocodile collided with him, Steve would yell out, "Thank God its mouth is closed!" I couldn't figure out why Steve was still in the water with nothing to protect him from the crocodile's bone-crunching jaws. Even though Steve had assured me that this relatively small crocodile would only try to bite in self-defense, I still desperately wanted him to get out of the water.

No sooner had I decided that this was just too difficult a task and Steve should get out, the spotlight began to glow orange. Without warning, the beam suddenly dimmed, and then blinked out. The inky blackness engulfed us all. My heart began to pound. I wasn't sure where I was, or if the water was even still in front of me. Someone didn't check the battery, I thought to myself.

Then I heard Steve's voice just in front of me as he angrily yelled, "Get a torch on me now!"

I heard a scuffle and then a small, pale beam was shining on Steve, standing perfectly motionless in the middle of the water. Without the benefit of a one-million-candle-power spotlight, the crocodile now had the advantage. Its vision would not have been impaired like ours when the lights went out, and it might have already slipped past Steve in the confusion. Steve had to know immediately what was going on and rushed forward.

The croc was there. It began flailing around in the shallow water. This time Steve got the net in its mouth and it bit down hard, snapping the stick. I could see the jagged outline of the crocodile's tail stir the surface of the water. Steve yelled for me to grab it. I froze for an instant—

Steve and I restrain an angry saltwater crocodile.

how exactly should I do that? Then I heard Steve's booming voice again, *"Now!"* I scrambled down the muddy embankment and grabbed the tail with both hands. It was smooth and soft, yet firm like muscle, and it was difficult to get a proper grip.

"Pull!" Steve commanded.

As we both struggled to drag the crocodile from the water, I couldn't believe its strength. One sideways swipe of its tail would knock me off balance and, try as I might, I couldn't keep it from spinning out of my grip as the croc death-rolled to try and escape. The rolling only made it more tangled in the net. Finally, we were able to drag the croc clear of the bank and fell on top of it, totally exhausted.

Tired and shaking, I hadn't realized that this job was only half over. Now we had to untangle this beautiful animal from what seemed like miles of fine-meshed net. The croc had everything from its toes to its teeth securely entwined. After removing the bulk of the net from its body, we had the tricky job of getting the mesh out of its mouth! Steve held the croc's head in his hands while he used the weight of his body, lying flat on the crocodile's back to keep it from thrashing and struggling. Then he gently loosened his grip on those powerful jaws, allowing them to open.

In just a few, short minutes all the netting was successfully removed and we positioned her in a coffin-shaped crocodile box for her transport back to the river.

Just after midnight, we reached the river. Steve had captured crocodiles in this section of the river many times over the last few years and he knew it like his own backyard. If this croc did turn out to be a female, as we suspected, she would fit right back into this ecosystem. Female crocodiles coexist with few arguments. But a big male saltwater crocodile will defend his territory from other males, even if it means a fight to the death. Steve had to be sure before we put this young crocodile back in the river.

As we slid back the top of the box, Steve dove his hands in to secure the crocodile at the back of her neck and prevent her from death rolling or biting

A subdued croc with top-jaw rope and blindfold.

someone. Together, we lifted her from the box and made sure her eyes were blindfolded to keep her calm while we examined her. At this point I queried Steve why he didn't sedate the crocodile to keep it calm and make handling safer. There in the dark, with a seven-foot crocodile between us, Steve took the time to explain that crocodiles metabolize drugs differently from mammals. He knew of people who had successfully sedated these giant reptiles, but sometimes a crocodile would never wake up. It was his own personal choice, and one I fully agreed with. I admired Steve even more for his willingness to risk his own well-being to protect the animals he loved.

After we finished taking some measurements of the crocodile, and Steve had confirmed that she was a female, we carried her right down to the water's edge. I stepped clear as Steve knelt over this crocodile for the last time.

"Goodbye, little girl," I heard him whisper. Then with a splash, she was gone. We drove in silence, alone with our thoughts, all the way back to camp.

The next morning we discussed that for the first time, the big croc we were after had taken a lead-in bait. Now it was only a matter of time and we'd catch her for sure.

After our big old crocodile had been taking lead-in baits regularly for about a week, Steve thought we would be safe filming around the trap site at night without scaring her off. One night we prepared the boats to go out after dark to see what we could film. We ate dinner in a hurry, as if that would make it dark quicker, and then sat around camp to wait. Steve wanted to be at the trap just before the moon came up. About 9 P.M. we headed out all right, but not to the trap.

More visitors arrived—two men who pulled up just on dark. Sui had been barking at them for about the last five minutes, ever since she first heard the truck approaching. The men looked a little bit concerned when Sui walked stiff-legged up to them, displaying her hackles.

Our visitors were fishermen. They enjoyed casting around a boat ramp a few miles downstream and had been fishing there for years, but lately had been having problems with crocodiles.

"But none of the crocodiles have territories that far downstream," Steve interjected.

The men nodded their heads and agreed with Steve. They knew there were no big crocs living in the vicinity, that's why they preferred to fish and camp at that particular spot. It was the smaller crocodiles, under six feet, that were bothering them. I couldn't figure out why little crocodiles would bother these men when they had grown up in crocodile country. Steve knew. He explained to the men that if they cleaned their fish at the boat ramp and dumped the fish frames

The spectacular wetland habitat of North Queensland.

in the water, the smaller crocodiles would figure out really quickly where to go for a free feed. Occasionally a little crocodile has been known to be so bold as to get hooked on a fishing line!

The men began to look a little uncomfortable and guilty, so Steve changed the subject a bit. Steve asked the men when they last saw the boldest of the troublemakers.

"That's why we're here," they replied. "It's waiting for us to dump our scraps now."

That was all Steve needed to hear. We were off to catch another crocodile.

I was quite surprised to discover that the little crocodiles at the boat ramp didn't zoom off when we approached, but rather casually retreated to the tangle of submerged mangrove roots. They didn't seem terribly worried about us at all. We scanned the water for the largest of these adolescent crocs to see if we could take him out first: Steve was quite confident that shifting the most curious

Steve and I spotlighting for crocs.

crocodile would be upsetting to the others and encourage them to be more wary. Although we must have counted half a dozen little fellows, the big boy didn't show himself.

Steve came up with another idea: maybe he could catch a couple of the smaller ones, and that would cause enough commotion to keep them all at bay and solve the problem. We all agreed to give it a go.

I knew the drill; I'd heard Steve talk about it during his crocodile demonstrations back at the Park a million times. I had just never actually done it before! I had been licensed for driving a boat, so I knew how to idle it up to a crocodile sitting in the water. When Steve spotted the first croc, I was ready. Steve positioned himself up at the front of the boat and held the bright spotlight on the little croc's eyes as we approached. The water was so full of silt, it was impossible to view the crocodile's body clearly. Steve determined whether or not it was small enough to jump solely by the size of its head.

As we cruised in on the croc, Steve gave me the thumbs-up and we were on. He passed the spotlight back to me and positioned himself at the bow of the boat. As he dove headfirst into the water, the boat was speared backward. I wasn't prepared for this and struggled to keep the light on target. A spluttering Steve surfaced. He was used to working on his own or with a more experienced driver. He didn't have to say anything—I knew why he'd missed. Next time my spotlight would be steady as a rock.

The crocodiles seemed to be playing a game of cat and mouse with us. They would surface near the boat and then silently disappear. I was eager to show Steve that I had learned from my first mistake and was getting impatient with these little rascals, which just would not hold still. Finally, I got my chance. As I idled the boat in to our next target, Steve was ready on the bow before he passed me the light. As he dove in, the boat shot backward, but this time I was ready. But it was clear that the croc saw Steve coming. Through no fault of mine, he missed again.

Jumping a crocodile is not simply a matter of flinging oneself off the bow of the boat and grabbing it. A good jump takes precision and timing. When Steve jumps a croc, he must aim right for the neck. His hands will push the crocodile's face away from his own to avoid a nasty bite. Steve's legs wrap around the crocodile's tail to keep it from swimming off with him. Here is the catch: if Steve were to aim for the crocodile's neck and the croc saw him coming, the crocodile would submerge. In order for the croc to submerge, it slips backward in the water first. Once it's under the water, the crocodile tucks its legs to its sides and uses that huge, powerful tail to propel it through the water nearly as fast as a dolphin! Therefore Steve tries to aim for the crocodile's mid-section—as the croc retreats, Steve lands precisely on its neck. This works really well unless the crocodile stays where it is. In which case, Steve could end up grabbing the croc mid-body, and the shocked crocodile could easily swing around and give Steve a nasty bite!

Steve missed a second crocodile, and as he spotted a third just ahead, I knew all these things would be going through his mind. And after two misses, Steve was eager to successfully nab this one. The ever-present camera wasn't helping.

I could see Steve's calf muscles flex as he steadied himself at the bow of the boat. I glanced down at the crocodile's head, just showing above the water. It sat motionless, suspended at a forty-five-degree angle in the water, thinking it was invisible. We were nearly on top of it now and Steve should have been handing me the spotlight. He hesitated as I reached forward, but finally passed the spotlight over.

As Steve dived over the front of the dinghy, both man and crocodile disappeared. Steve must have met his mark. I tried to remain calm—I knew that the crocodile would be trying to

Catching and restraining crocodiles is dirty work.

lodge Steve on the rocks and snags at the bottom of the river. Any moment now, Steve would bounce off the bottom and flip the croc straight in the boat. I had to be ready to jump it as soon as it was in. As I strained to see into the murky water, two silhouettes churned below. Steve was really struggling.

Something was terribly wrong. Steve's head broke the surface of the water. He gasped for air and tried to yell something to me as he was pulled back into the river. Steve clearly needed help. I had no idea what else to do but abandon the boat and jump in. I immediately reached out to grab hold of something. I felt the familiar smoothness of the crocodile's tail. Steve had not managed to grip the croc's tail between his legs and now we were both being towed into deeper water. But Steve was at least able to get air and, exhausted, he practically pleaded with me to swim for the bank. I kicked through the water with all my strength, but what was difficult to control on dry land was impossible to control in the water. This crocodile was in its own territory. I was overwhelmed by its sheer power and force as I struggled to find my footing. Under the water, the riverbank floor was steep and silty. The mangrove mud was just too slippery to climb with this aquatic predator thrashing in my arms. Steve could feel the bottom, too, now. He swung the crocodile's head toward shore and coached me like a drill sergeant.

"Get up there, babe, get up there!" he urged over and over. I concentrated on his voice as I planted each foot in the mud and strained to gain ground. Letting go was not an option. The crocodile would not retreat without giving one of us a good, solid bite. This crocodile was far too large to risk that! Once we cleared the water, the crocodile would be out of his element. We struggled on a few steps and then fell on him in a heap. Steve, still gasping for air, repeated the obvious.

"Too big, too big," he kept saying. I couldn't agree more! Without hesitation, Steve asked me for a blindfold. His first concern was for the well-being of this poor, frightened crocodile.

Since I had left the blindfolds on the boat, Steve instructed me to tear off his shirt as he held the croc down. After a bit of effort and a few torn-off buttons, we could feel the croc relax a little as his whole world went dark. Next, Steve decided to secure the croc's jaws. Ordinarily, we would never tie a crocodile's mouth shut. If under stress the croc brought up his last meal,

Steve and me restraining an alligator prior to relocation within the Park.

he would drown in his own regurgitation. Not a pleasant thought. But Steve and I were just too fatigued to risk holding him in the boat, so we agreed to rope his jaws for the short trip. Rope was something I did have. Whether it was crocs or pigs, it seemed I was constantly needing a bit of rope!

Once we were safely back in the boat, Steve was elated. What a capture! Not only had we rescued this curious crocodile, we'd also strengthened the bond between us. We both knew that, in years to come, we'd face many more dangerous situations and we knew beyond a shadow of a doubt that we could count on each other.

We all agreed that we were definitely on a roll, so the following night we would try our luck at the trap site.

The sounds on the river change when the sun goes down. The familiar daytime wildlife is replaced with unfamiliar bumps in the night. The most disconcerting of all these nighttime creatures are, surprisingly, the fish. One particular species seems to enjoy flinging itself into the air. This night, with incredible lack of control, these little beasties occasionally sailed straight into the boat! As we approached the trap, Steve slipped the engine into neutral and took a few minutes to thoroughly survey the area. As I cautiously peered down the beam of the dim light, it was precisely at that moment that one of these little fish decided to do its impersonation of a sea-to-air missile. *Thump!* Direct hit—right into the side of my head! I'm proud to say that I didn't scream. In spite of the fact that I was deep in thought about crocodiles, and had no idea what had attacked me, I didn't cry out. I did, however, nearly tip the boat over as I practically jumped out of my skin! Stupid fish.

Needless to say, Steve was not overly impressed with this latest example of my stealth in the bush. I resolved to myself that, no matter what happened, I would not overreact. That's why as we approached the trap, I remained cool, calm, and collected in the face of our next nocturnal visitor. Steve was thrilled. There, hanging down in front of us, was a very happy carpet python. Inevitably, the bait at the croc trap attracts more than just crocodiles. This python was probably hoping to cash in on some of the rats hanging around the dangling pork. But tonight, the pork was gone. Since we'd arrived too late to catch a glimpse of our big saltie, we decided to film this pretty little carpet snake instead and call it a night.

Steve idled in close, then caught the branch that the python

Steve handles another visitor, the venomous taipan.

was hanging on to help stop the boat. As I tried to appear casual about the whole encounter, the snake decided to swing out for a better look at me. Even though I understood that the snake was harmless, instinctively I leaned backward, out of strike range. Dangerous or not, I wasn't too keen on the thought of being bitten on the face! As I leaned back, the boat shifted. We were both standing up now, and as Steve got a better grip on the limb to steady the boat, I heard a loud crack!

As the limb broke, everything was suddenly off balance. I felt myself falling with nothing in front of me to grab hold of. I went over the side and plummeted like a stone into the water. Eyes open wide, I can vividly remember the darkness of the silty water all around me. Directly above me was a light, like a beacon in a dark alley. I swam up toward it, easing myself through the water. Then I realized I was in the water directly in front of the trap site where a large saltwater crocodile had been bold enough to snatch a lead-in bait less than an hour ago! She could have been right next to me and I would have had no hope of seeing her. I tried desperately to push these thoughts out of my mind.

Don't panic! I practically screamed to myself. Don't panic and don't thrash around like an injured animal. I popped up to see Steve, the cameraman, and the boat drifting down the river. I was losing the boat. This couldn't be happening! I didn't dare swim, I was terrified just to tread water. I could see Steve ripping at the outboard motor. It wouldn't start! I called to him, but he was swearing loudly at the engine.

I tried to stop thinking, but my horrible imagination wouldn't shut off. I waited for the sensation of teeth piercing my flesh. I knew the crocodile would first grab my leg and that with the kind of pressure its jaws exerted, my leg would be crushed. I would have no hope of escape. I began choking on my words as I cried out to Steve. If he could just get the outboard to turn over—crocodiles are very shy of the sound.

I saw Steve, in ultimate frustration, punch the outboard as hard as he could. It started with the next pull. As Steve helped me into the boat I thought I was going to throw up. I couldn't appreciate the panic that had gone on in the boat. Even the cameraman violated his basic rule: he stopped filming! He actually put the camera down and stopped rolling, but there was nothing he could do to help. And as he started filming again, he was faced with his own fears. Extremely phobic of snakes, he well knew that there was a carpet python sitting in the bottom of the boat where it had fallen with the limb. I began to settle down and even had a bit of a laugh as I sat across from the cameraman perched high on a box to avoid the still-loose snake.

After all the commotion at the trap site, Steve figured the crocodile would be too disturbed to return for a while. Much to Steve's surprise, she took a lead-in bait the very next night. Since we were faced with leaving camp anyway to restock our supplies, Steve thought he'd take a chance and bait the trap. He put a huge chunk of rotting meat in the back of the trap, fastened to the trigger mechanism. The lead-in bait was removed and I got to help mask our scent by rubbing pig entrails all around the trap. According to the swarms of meat ants, I must have done a good job! Now that the trap was set, we stayed right off the river for the rest of the day. Steve wanted to make sure that nothing would disturb this old girl.

That night we hardly slept, waiting and wondering what was going on at the trap. In

Steve examines a croc slide on the river bank.

the morning, Steve forced himself to wait until the sun was just about to come up over the horizon. When we left camp on high tide, no one knew what to expect. As we rounded the final bend in the river, Steve wasn't looking for the trap, he was looking in the trees. Sure enough, the weight bag was no longer visible. It had been triggered. Something was in the trap!

I was out of the boat first and could see a shape in the trap. While I tied up the boat, Steve edged his way to the back of the trap. It was her! She uttered a low growl, almost like a roar, as we approached her. She must have been caught several hours earlier. All the vegetation around her had been flattened and she was very muddy. In the light of day, and on dry ground, I didn't feel as frightened of her. Actually, I felt sorry for her. This had been her home for probably thirty to fifty years, and now she had to move or risk the poacher's gun.

Steve's first concern was regulating her body temperature. Now that the sun was up, she would normally be back in the water. She'd then have the option to stay cool, or bask in the sun for short periods. Steve instructed me to start hauling buckets of water to pour over her in an attempt to keep her body temperature at a comfortable 30°C (86°F). Next, we began cutting the ropes from the weight bag so we could more easily manipulate both crocodile and trap. Steve worked quickly around the crocodile, familiar with exactly what to do. As he instructed me, and assisted the film crew, I was struck by the thought that Steve routinely used to do all of this on his own.

When everything was ready and the crocodile looked stable, it was time to manipulate her out of the trap and into the boat. Steve reminded me how important it was to react instantly to his instructions. Any hesitation could prove to be a fatal mistake.

The first step was to secure a top-jaw rope on the crocodile. Steve gently eased a stick with a rope tied to it through the croc's mouth. He nimbly tied the rope over the crocodile's top jaw, being careful to make sure the rope was securely wedged between those enormous teeth. When the top-jaw rope was tied off to a tree, the crocodile's movement was minimized and Steve could begin removing the trap, tail end first. This worked well for a while, but Steve really needed to have her movement restricted even more.

"You will have to jump on her head," Steve stated matter-of-factly.

It was one thing to help restrain smaller crocs, but as I looked down at this giant dinosaur, I wasn't sure if I could actually bring myself to lie down on her head! She began to struggle and, lightning fast, Steve was on her.

It was now or never, so I eased in next to Steve and tried to get my fingers around the crocodile's massive jaws to keep her mouth shut. I could feel her large, bony scutes scattered down her back as they dug into my ribs. As Steve worked to remove the net, my fingers ached from hanging on so tightly. In spite of the discomfort, I was awestruck. In the beginning I had admired Steve for the courage it took to work so closely with these ancient saurians—now I was doing it, too. It was certainly a proud moment to be part of the team, rescuing this amazing creature.

Just as my legs began to cramp, and I wasn't sure how much longer I could hold on, Steve was ready to remove her head from the trap. Throughout this entire ordeal, the crocodile had never given up. Periodically, she would build up to the point where I knew she was going to struggle. Tired as she was, it would still take both of us to hold her until she settled back down again. Removing the last bit of net was the most dangerous time for Steve and me. Steve had to untie her top-jaw rope from the tree and feed the rope through the net. As the last of the mesh came away from her face she was completely free of any restraints. Steve and I, alone, were holding her there.

A quick measurement indicated that she was about ten feet long. As a crocodile grows, for every twelve inches they increase their length, they gain another thirty-three percent in body weight. We could only estimate, but she probably weighed in at around 390 pounds—nearly double Steve's weight!

Now we had to carry/drag her to the river's edge and load her into the boat. As we neared the water, the croc could sense freedom. All she wanted to do was go home. Steve and I were quite shocked when we saw the boat. We hadn't taken into consideration the dropping tide. There below us, about twelve feet down, was the tiny dinghy. Now what do we do? Without skipping a beat Steve said to me, "Let me have her." Then, throwing his arms around her neck and a leg over her back, Steve literally rode the crocodile straight over the edge, landing in the boat with a bang!

Both Steve and the crocodile were fine. I slid down the steep embankment and jumped in to give Steve a hand. The croc didn't like it a bit when the motor started, but once we were under way it was a quick trip to the release site. Just as well. It would be quite easy to suffer a broken arm or leg while trying to restrain a thrashing croc in the boat.

This tributary was quite remote. It had a lovely sand bar for sunning and high

A warning to travelers heading inland from the relative safety of Australia's coastal region.

ground for nesting. Our girl would be quite happy and undisturbed here. We eased her out of the boat and set her next to the water. She seemed surprised when we finally let her go. She looked around for a moment before walking toward the water. A bit cumbersome and awkward on land, the crocodile became poetry in motion when she entered the water.

Emotions ran high as we watched her gracefully disappear. None of us could say a word. We had not managed to save her mate from the cruel fate of a poacher's bullet, but she was safe now and she would make a life without him. I could not imagine what would make someone shoot this magnificent predator. For sixty-five million years they have lived on this planet. Now humans controlled their fate. I hoped with all my heart that we could one day make people understand that crocodiles are not monsters. They are good mothers and passionate lovers. They live over one hundred years and have an intricate family structure. I wouldn't want to live in a world where there were no crocodiles. It would be like removing the river's soul.

We packed up quickly (Steve does everything in a hurry) and headed back for home at the Park. I didn't fully appreciate then that this was just the beginning. Over the following years Steve and I would spend about half our lives in the bush. We didn't realize just how well received our wildlife documentaries would be.

We were not back long when it was "on the road again," and in the next four years we covered a lot of ground in order to film fifteen wildlife documentaries. I reckon I have gotten to know Australia better than most Australians! This is a beautiful country with spectacular wildlife, but how little we really know about the unique flora and fauna that live here. We've unlocked some secrets, but a great deal remains a mystery.

My most memorable filming experience, and closest call, occurred on the way to Queensland's Simpson Desert. Steve and I were on a mission to capture a male perentie lizard for our lonely female perenties back at the Park. The expedition would also prove to give us enough footage for a two-part television special entitled "Crocodile Hunter Goes West."

En route, Steve took advantage as always of any wildlife filming opportunities. This time we stopped to camp at a series of fantastic gorges.

Scenes from our adventures on one of Australia's beautiful river systems.

Perentie.

Steve bounded down the steep embankments to see what secrets these caverns held and twice he returned with the bleached bones of animals that had become trapped in the areas with sheer walls, impossible to escape. We agreed to try and film in the deepest area we could find.

It was one thing for Steve and me to abseil down for a quick look, but quite another to assemble crew, camera gear, and sound equipment. It took seven hours of hard yakka and numerous trips before we were set up to film at about three hundred feet from the bottom. This last drop would have to be made by Steve and myself on our own. It was then that we discovered our cameraman wasn't keen on heights. He was absolutely paralyzed at the thought of leaning over that cliff to film our descent. Luckily, one of our crew was an experienced mountaineer who agreed to help the cameraman back up to a tree where he could be strapped up in a full body harness and made to feel secure. With a little additional coaching, he could film over the edge with no problem.

That would work fine for a wide shot, but to follow us into the chasm we would need to

rig up a special miniature camera on a long cord. Steve and I practiced with it until we were confident of handling the descent and the camera. Finally, with the afternoon shadows getting critically long, we were ready to drop into the unknown.

It should be mentioned that I have only ever seen one other fellow climb like Steve. His name was Archie, and he lived at Taronga Zoo. He just happened to be an orangutan! Therefore, my heart only mildly skipped a beat as I watched Steve free climb around the bulging rock face with only the smallest toeholds. The big difference was, this time I had to follow!

The plan was to free climb down to a larger ledge Steve had seen below. This lower ledge would afford us the luxury of good tie-off points so we could abseil all the way to the bottom. As I approached the tiny ledge where we would start our climb down, I felt a tightness in my chest as my breathing came quicker. I tried to relax, but the first part of our climb would be over vertical.

I knew that I had to calm down or I would be in trouble. Every climber knows that the skill is about seventy-five percent mental. Confidence is everything. I tried to concentrate on Steve's instructions, but he could see that I wasn't comfortable with the situation at all. In order to give me that all-important mental advantage, Steve tied me off to the only thing available . . . himself. That

Steve abseiling in a gorge during one of our filming expeditions.

rope connecting me to Steve gave me the courage to ease myself out on the tiny ledge and over the edge.

I was feeling with my toes for a foothold and it quickly became apparent that my short legs could not follow the same pathway that Steve had when he first checked out this route. For a brief moment I felt the security of a tiny toehold. As I wedged the tip of my hiking boot into the crack, my weight shifted to bring my other leg down and without warning, I felt as if someone had suddenly jerked me downward as the rock abruptly crumbled away from under my foot.

I remember thinking what an odd sensation it was. I was falling, but not like the character of some movie hurtling over a cliff. Rather, I was very undramatically leaving all the skin from my thighs on the rock face as I slid straight down. I couldn't scramble. I was over vertical. In one swift instant I was hanging on by my hands. All thoughts of the miniature camera, still filming beside us, went out of my head. I knew that I was in big trouble when I heard the fear in Steve's voice. "Just hang on and I'll get you," he ordered. But as he leaned over to grab my arms, I was just out of reach.

By now I was too tired to pull myself up and the muscles in my arms were beginning to cramp. "Hang on or you'll pull us both over!" Steve yelled. I was painfully aware of the fact that we were tied together. Try as I might, I didn't have the strength to pull myself up with one arm so that I could grab Steve's hand. I was terrified to feel my grip slipping. It made no difference now whether or not I'd been tied to Steve—I simply couldn't hold on any longer. I slid further down the rock wall and dangled like a puppet at the end of the rope.

Steve was lying completely flat now, at a dangerous angle over the edge. I was practically sobbing as I begged him to pull me up. "Give me your hand, I can reach you," I heard Steve's strained voice say. As I reached up, I didn't even have the strength to close my hand around his. Steve stretched out to the very limit and clamped his hand around my wrist. With a power that must have been pure adrenaline, he dragged me up to the ledge until he could

grasp my harness with his other hand. We lay right there on that ledge for what seemed like an eternity. Not until I had begun to regain my composure did I notice the crew scrambling down to help us. They had been with the cameraman the whole time, coaching him through his bout with vertigo!

I'm happy to report that I've been on many climbs since, without incident!

The trip to the desert held many other adventures, not the least of which included capturing the big male perentie we were after. The perentie lives in some of the most remote desert areas in Australia, frequenting certain mesas and rocky outcroppings where it can escape the extreme temperatures in caves and hollows. On this particular trip the temperature would soar to 50°C (122°F) by smoko, which is our traditional morning tea break. By afternoon, the only living things moving were the five billion flies trying to pile into my eyes, nose, and mouth.

A newly hatched perentie.

It had been decided that we'd head out to search for this giant lizard (the largest in Australia) when the temperature was still a relatively "cool" 30°C (86°F). Knowing how secretive this spotted giant can be, I was totally shocked when Steve spied one in the open at the base of a pile of boulders. He must have been out foraging and was focusing on something to eat rather than potential dangers. In fact, I don't know what this lizard would have considered dangerous. He was massive. He would have been nearly seven feet long. As he turned to size us up, I began to appreciate why the

Steve with a perentie back at the Park.

Aborigines refer to perenties as "land crocodiles." He wasn't about to turn tail and run away from us.

I felt very intimidated, but Steve knew just what to do. He approached the perentie without looking him in the eye. That seemed to be some sort of predator "rule" which enabled Steve to approach him. When Steve was close enough, he began a sort of stand-off with the varanid. If Steve moved in too close I would hear the telltale hiss, which is reptile for "bug off!" This, along with some vicious tail slaps, went on for some time. Finally, Steve faked out the angry reptile by reaching for him with one hand while grabbing him with the other.

I'm proud to report that the female perenties back at the park fell desperately in love with this hunk of a lizard and reproduce quite nicely every year. Steve takes the perentie breeding

Steve always handles all spiders with great care.

With the exception of the Sydney funnel web, all spider bites should be treated by applying ice (wrapped in a towel) directly to the bite site until reaching the hospital. Because of the nature of the venom, bites from Sydney funnel web spiders should be treated with a pressure bandage. Remember, if you don't have a pressure bandage handy, remove clothing and make one!

Although a tourniquet is not usually recommended because it cuts off circulation, in some situations it can become necessary. In the case of a hemorrhaging wound, say from a shark bite, a tourniquet may be essential. A gaping wound may require packing with, for example, a rolled-up shirt. Direct pressure will help stop the flow of blood and must be maintained until reaching the hospital.

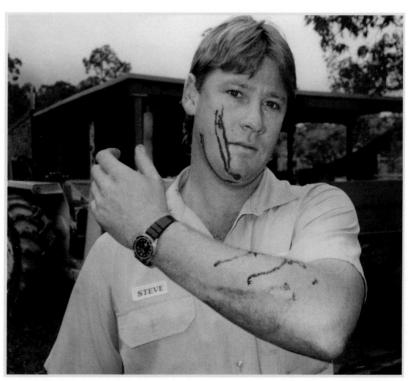
Steve after being bitten by a nonvenomous snake.

Australia's Dingo Fence—the world's longest man-made structure.

Although sharks seem scary, in Australia shark strikes kill fewer people than anything else except crocodiles! (That's fewer than one person per year.)

One of our most challenging projects was filming the world's longest man-made structure. Australia's Dingo Fence is even longer than the Great Wall of China. Stretching more than three thousand miles and with little more than a track to follow, it took us over three weeks just to drive from end to end. With special permission from landowners as well as permits from government departments, we were able to see for ourselves just how this dog fence works.

The objective, of course, is to keep sheep on one side and Australia's wild dog, the dingo, on the other. We discovered, however, that the fence affected other animals as well. Everything from kangaroos to emus and even wombats and willy wag tails have conflicts with the monumental fenceline.

We had problems of our own. In some areas where water pooled from rain showers far away, the fenceline was actually underwater. On more than one occasion, Steve had to walk through waist-deep water to find out if the track was passable at all. In one particular section, the rain had turned the track into a muddy slick. As the crew's vehicle rounded a corner we watched as it slid, as if in slow motion, straight into the fence. The graziers were amazingly polite about the whole thing as they set about repairing the significant hole left in the fence!

Later that night the weather set in so dramatically that we didn't dare stop to set camp, as the water was rising fast. We picked our way cautiously along the slippery flooded track. After an incredibly long ten hours, we had gained a mere sixty miles. We secured a patch of high ground and grabbed some much-needed rest.

A significant portion of the trip was quite depressing. If a dingo was shot it was customary to hang it on the fence. Whichever side of the fence it was hanging on indicated the side on which it was shot. Some of the carcasses had been hanging on the fence so long they had mummified. Others bore the evidence of being scalped for the bounty that is still paid for each dingo killed.

All in all, the reception of our wildlife documentaries has been a bit overwhelming. To date, our series has gone to air in over thirty countries, most recently in the United States. It has been a real honor to have been so widely

Another sad trophy for dingo bounty hunters.

accepted. If Steve and I can demonstrate how marvelous it is to work so closely with nature, we have a chance of encouraging others to join in to help. Children have been the most enthusiastic.

The filming continues. Steve and I joke that as long as our legs still work, we will press on. The other life forms we share this planet with are exciting, vibrant, interesting creatures, and Steve and I are determined to show how important wildlife conservation is to them and to us.

Perentie.

Steve bounded down the steep embankments to see what secrets these caverns held and twice he returned with the bleached bones of animals that had become trapped in the areas with sheer walls, impossible to escape. We agreed to try and film in the deepest area we could find.

It was one thing for Steve and me to abseil down for a quick look, but quite another to assemble crew, camera gear, and sound equipment. It took seven hours of hard yakka and numerous trips before we were set up to film at about three hundred feet from the bottom. This last drop would have to be made by Steve and myself on our own. It was then that we discovered our cameraman wasn't keen on heights. He was absolutely paralyzed at the thought of leaning over that cliff to film our descent. Luckily, one of our crew was an experienced mountaineer who agreed to help the cameraman back up to a tree where he could be strapped up in a full body harness and made to feel secure. With a little additional coaching, he could film over the edge with no problem.

That would work fine for a wide shot, but to follow us into the chasm we would need to make people understand that crocodiles are not monsters. They are good mothers and passionate lovers. They live over one hundred years and have an intricate family structure. I wouldn't want to live in a world where there were no crocodiles. It would be like removing the river's soul.

We packed up quickly (Steve does everything in a hurry) and headed back for home at the Park. I didn't fully appreciate then that this was just the beginning. Over the following years Steve and I would spend about half our lives in the bush. We didn't realize just how well received our wildlife documentaries would be.

We were not back long when it was "on the road again," and in the next four years we covered a lot of ground in order to film fifteen wildlife documentaries. I reckon I have gotten to know Australia better than most Australians! This is a beautiful country with spectacular wildlife, but how little we really know about the unique flora and fauna that live here. We've unlocked some secrets, but a great deal remains a mystery.

My most memorable filming experience, and closest call, occurred on the way to Queensland's Simpson Desert. Steve and I were on a mission to capture a male perentie lizard for our lonely female perenties back at the Park. The expedition would also prove to give us enough footage for a two-part television special entitled "Crocodile Hunter Goes West."

En route, Steve took advantage as always of any wildlife filming opportunities. This time we stopped to camp at a series of fantastic gorges.

Scenes from our adventures on one of Australia's beautiful river systems.

Chapter VIII

God's Twenty Acres

Wildlife documentary filming on location continues to be one exciting adventure after another, but the foundation of everything we do is definitely at Beerwah in Queensland, at our zoo. And daily life there can be anything from business dilemmas to wildlife dramas. I certainly never get bored waking up each morning and wondering, What will happen today?

When Steve and I first took over running the zoo we were eager to make his parents proud of our work. One of the first projects we took on together concerned Harriet, our giant Galapagos land tortoise, which we believed to be of the subspecies *Geochelone elephantopus guntheri*. We also believed that she had been brought to Australia some 130 years earlier on a whaling ship. It was not unusual for the whaling fleets to load up large numbers of these gentle giants as they passed the Galapagos Islands on the way to Australia from the Americas, the tortoises serving as a source of much-needed fresh meat during their three-month journey. Those taken onboard the whalers would be butchered one by one as they

Studying tortoise behavior can be dirty work.

were needed. It was thought that, somehow, Harriet escaped the knife and ended up as someone's pet before taking up residence at the City Botanic Gardens in Brisbane, around the turn of the century.

We were quite comfortable with Harriet's story and quoted her history at our daily giant tortoise demonstrations, but then we met up with Scott Thompson, one of Australia's leading tortoise experts. Everyone who encounters our 400-pound Harriet is impressed, but Scott was overwhelmed. He came up from Canberra on more than one occasion to study our old girl and felt that she didn't match the story we had been told about her.

After taking many measurements and even more photographs, Scott was convinced that Harriet was not a *G. e. guntheri,* but rather a *G. e. porteri.* Steve and I were excited at the thought of Harriet having some unusual history that might actually be documented somewhere and we gratefully enlisted Scott's help to research her story.

Our first step was the discovery that new DNA work on tortoises was being conducted in the United States at Texas A & M University. There, Ed Lewis was developing baselines from wild-bred tortoises on the Galapagos Islands, and these would enable identification through comparison of DNA of purebred subspecies in captivity. This was exciting news that meant we could scientifically determine exactly what Harriet was.

Harriet—Darwin's tortoise.

Another development came about when Scott Thompson visited the Queensland Museum in Brisbane to gather more tortoise data. By luck he came upon a giant tortoise preserved in spirit at the back of the museum's storage warehouse. Scott couldn't properly identify the tortoise as it was stored upside down. After turning the crate over, Scott discovered these words carved on the giant shell: "Tom—giant Galapagos land tortoise died 1929 Brisbane Botanic Gardens."

Scott couldn't believe his eyes. This preserved tortoise substantiated a newspaper article he'd seen reporting on three giant Galapagos tortoises brought to Australia in 1841 for the Brisbane Botanic Gardens. Two had died in the 1920s. Scott was sure Tom must have been one of them. Perhaps Harriet was the third tortoise? If that were true, it would be incredible. The three tortoises had been collected in 1835 by Charles Darwin, and if Harriet was the survivor

Steve and me with Fijian crested iguanas.

she would be the oldest documented giant land tortoise in the world. This news just made it all the harder to wait for Ed Lewis and his all-important DNA work to be completed!

My experiences at the zoo continued to be a crash course in everything reptilian, my initial responsibilities including the baby crocodiles and the baby goannas. The little lizards were my favorites. They thought they were very tough and would tail-whip me violently every time I cleaned or fed them. My charges included everything from perenties to sand goannas and even the sleek little mertens water monitors. Although I was also learning to handle the adult versions of these species, I wasn't yet skilled enough to handle full-grown crocodiles and alligators on my own—or so I thought!

My graduation course with large adult alligators came quite unexpectedly. A friend of mine was over from Oregon for a visit. She has always been a big wildlife fan and had worked with me for several years at the emergency veterinary hospital. Now she was going to fulfill a dream by volunteering to work at our zoo for a few weeks to learn more about Australian fauna.

Dawn arrived tired after a tedious twenty-hour flight and I assured her that she would be feeling better after a good night's sleep. In the morning I'd show her how to clean and feed our eighteen species of bird. Dawn was only too happy to start her experiences Down Under with our sweet little kookaburras and tawny frog-mouths!

Steve was especially restless that night and had trouble getting any sleep. He is always alert to anything unusual going on, but even after checking the entire zoo grounds shortly after midnight, he couldn't find anything wrong. He finally got up for the day's work just after 4 A.M., while it was still dark. I didn't even hear him leave.

Suddenly, I was jarred awake when the door slammed open. "It's the alligators, come quick!" Steve was yelling. I leapt out of bed and started scrambling for my clothes with no idea what was going on. "Just put your shoes on and hurry!" Steve shouted over his shoulder as he ran out the door. I pounded on Dawn's door as I laced up my shoes and she dutifully raced after me in her pajamas as we hurried toward the alligator enclosure.

Fighting alligators can make quite a mess.

As we got to the outer safety fence, I couldn't believe my eyes. Locked together in mortal combat were our two largest female alligators, aptly named the Fang Sisters. Their jaws were clamped down on each other's head in some sort of dispute. Their small, peglike teeth were even puncturing skull and there was blood everywhere. Obstinate as bulldogs, they were not letting go! It would be hours before the staff would start arriving and these girls were busy trying to pull each other's head off *right now*.

Steve was over the two fencelines in an instant, so Dawn and I followed him in. "Terri, you jump on that one and, Dawn, jump the other one," Steve instructed. "Hold onto their heads while I get their jaws apart." Luckily, Dawn didn't even have time to think and she followed my lead, lying down flat across the alligator and hugging its head tightly to minimize movement. The alligators were growing tired from all their struggling but it still took Steve some time to pry them apart. He finally had to stand on the lower jaw of one of the Fang Sisters and use both hands to pull her teeth up and out of the head of the other. But once he had them separated, they immediately swung around to start fighting again.

Dawn and I jumped clear as Steve pulled one of the alligators by the tail in order to move her away from the conflict. Like a giant wind-up toy, she'd then plod back toward her sister, and Steve would have to pull her back again. I turned to a wide-eyed Dawn and said, "Welcome to Australia!" She was speechless.

Later, after the staff had arrived, we discovered the cause of our alligators' conflict. Like a chicken, a female alligator will produce eggs even if she has had no contact with a male. Our girls had built nests in the exact same spot and then proceeded to defend their nests, and their unfertilized eggs, against each other. To this day we have to make sure the Fang Sisters don't build a nest or, as a consequence, lay their eggs. Their bodies then simply reabsorb the eggs and all conflict is avoided.

Our zoo work is not just limited to our own facility. We work with zoos around the world consulting on wildlife husbandry techniques that we are particularly experienced with. And, of course, because of the specialized nature of our zoo we're called upon quite often to help out with crocodiles. Whether a zoo is designing a new enclosure or just has some medical questions, we are always happy to lend our expertise. One of the most frequent requests for help comes when a crocodile needs to be moved.

One of the more challenging requests came from an aquarium in far North Queensland. The situation was not an unusual one; that of a saltwater crocodile that had outgrown his enclosure. Charlie had been hatched at a crocodile farm and, when he was about ten years old, instead of being turned into a pair of boots, he'd been lucky enough to find a home at the aquarium. For the past ten years he had lived there in a tidal pond. High besser block walls surrounded him on the rocky edge of the shoreline. Each day a piece of food was lowered over the wall on a line and tourists could experience his immense power as jaws snapped together over the food item. But the aquarium owners knew this was only a temporary home for Charlie. He was now over eleven feet long and weighed in at 705 pounds. He was growing too large for his pen and he just wasn't happy anymore.

Charlie had never been able to swim in deep water or feel mud between his toes. He couldn't see beyond the walls of his enclosure and he was getting bored with his feeding routine. Actually, "bored" probably doesn't correctly describe

Charlie.

his attitude. It was more like "angry." The owners of the aquarium asked if we could take him. Finding a good home for an animal that can grow to over twenty feet long and weigh well over a ton isn't easy. If no other zoo could be found to take Charlie he might have to be sent back to the farm. After many long discussions Steve and I agreed to take him, and preparations for his arrival at our park began.

The first step was to design and build Charlie's new enclosure. Because he was a mature male he couldn't be housed with any other male crocs or they would just fight for territory. We decided not to risk putting him in with a female, either. He hadn't seen another crocodile for more than a decade, so we couldn't know how he would react. We finally decided on a section of pond that could be barricaded off and began to build.

First Steve put up a visual barrier between Charlie's pond and the crocodile next door.

Charlie in his old concrete enclosure, awaiting relocation to a more natural site at the Park.

Steve and Wes trying to secure a top-jaw rope on Charlie.

This was crucial as Charlie's new neighbor would be Acco, the largest croc at the zoo. With Acco more than sixteen feet long and weighing in at one ton, we didn't want Charlie trying to pick a fight through the fence! Next, Steve began placing the steel bars that separated the pond into two sections. This was the tricky part. Steve had his welding equipment in our crocodile dinghy, floating in the middle of the pond. I sat by the plug. If Steve were to get an electrical shock it was my job to unplug him!

Finally, the last touches were added to Charlie's new home. There were tea trees for shade and lamandra grass to hide in. There was a main pond as well as a little billabong. Everything was designed to make Charlie feel that he was living out in the bush.

Then it was a question of how to catch Charlie and remove him from his present pen. The tall walls that surrounded him posed unique problems. We couldn't get in with him unless it was low tide and, even then, once in there was no way to jump back out quickly! Steve decided to utilize most of our staff and leave the zoo to run with a skeleton crew. We even enlisted the help of Bruce, our local excavator driver, who could provide that extra boost when it came time to lift 705 pounds of crocodile over the eight-foot wall. We were lucky enough to have Steve's parents to help out, too.

We all arrived at the aquarium at low tide, as planned. Charlie seemed to know something was up as he sat at the far end of his enclosure. Ladders were placed over the sides and Steve began to try to top-jaw rope Charlie from the top of the wall. Not only did Steve's

Steve holding an alligator.

attempts fail, they made Charlie even more nervous. In order to position the rope accurately, Steve had no choice but to climb in. Charlie seemed shocked to see someone on his level for the first time in years. This gave Steve the chance he needed and he quickly secured the first top-jaw rope.

Steve, Wes, and me being filmed while loading Charlie into a transport box.

Once Charlie realized he was caught, he became furious. Holding the rope on top of the wall, Bob, Steve's father, tried to keep the thrashing crocodile from grabbing Steve. Steve was dancing around Charlie's snapping jaws trying to secure another rope. Sensing that Steve needed help, Wes Mannion vaulted over the wall and ran up to the crocodile to distract him. Wes's plan worked perfectly. As Charlie swung around, mouth open, trying to kill Wes, Steve easily tossed the second rope over Charlie's top jaw.

Now that he was being pulled from two directions, Charlie couldn't swing his head. Meanwhile, the rest of the staff were poised on the edge of the wall, waiting for Steve to give the word. "You're in!" Steve yelled. I slid over the wall and dropped to the ground along with ten other people. We lined up behind the crocodile without saying a word. Charlie began to death roll. Once, twice...

"Go!" Steve shouted. Like a well-rehearsed rugby tackle, eleven bodies landed on Charlie. Steve eased himself off Charlie's head as Bob came down the ladder. Bob secured Charlie's jaws as he'd done with crocodiles a hundred times before. After we slid Charlie into his box, his jaw ropes were relaxed for his long drive home. After hoisting his heavy box over the wall, we all took a moment to revel in the attention being given by the press. Wet and muddy, we all still managed to smile for the cameras!

After a quick stop at the local truck scales to verify Charlie's weight, we were back home with him safe and sound. All hands were on deck as we slid Charlie out of his box and faced him toward his new pond.

When Steve gave the word, we all jumped off Charlie and ran. As usual, Steve was the last off and as he released Charlie's head, it was as if Charlie was finally free. He slid into the deep, dark, dirty water and completely disappeared. For the first time in his life, Charlie got to be a crocodile. We silently slipped away from his territory, leaving him to his camouflage in the reeds.

For the next few weeks Charlie was absolutely delirious with joy. He finally had the chance to be a predator and he hunted everything. He proceeded to kill as many fish, eels, yabbies, and turtles as he could find in his pond and then he turned his sights on land animals. Steve and I would laugh so hard, we'd have to sit down or we would have fallen over. Charlie would sit on the bank with the end of his tail twitching like a cat's as he stalked various birds and lizards. Of course, he didn't have a hope of catching anything as he lurched forward, awkwardly lunging for his prey. The lizards would just scurry out of his way and look at him as if to say, "What on earth do you think you're doing?"

Even now, Charlie is the only crocodile that we don't hand-feed. He has this habit of ignoring the food in your hand and aiming for the buttons on your shirt!

The director of our wildlife documentaries had noticed that some of our wildest adventures happened at home, and so was born the idea for "Sleeping With Crocodiles." Our usual filming trips were always lengthy affairs travelwise, and it was a real luxury to be filming in our own backyard. Working with some of the more dangerous animals proved to be an added bonus for me and pushed me into learning a little faster. When I watch this show today, I have to laugh. Some of the situations that scared me then are routine now.

The most rewarding experience I had was getting to know our boa constrictors. These huge snakes had never been handled and were just as afraid of me as I was of them. The big difference was, when they got scared enough, they would bite!

I decided to start small and work my way up. Steve had two young boa constrictors that lived in a large tank in the living room. I asked Steve's advice on the best way to become comfortable with them. He suggested I pick up one of the four-year-old snakes and get to know it by spending an hour or so with it every evening. I wasn't quite sure what I was supposed to do with it, but I chose the female and named her Rosie.

Our first evening was like an awkward date. Rosie sat coiled up at one end of the sofa looking as if she'd rather be anywhere else and I sat at the other end of the sofa trying to eat dinner. We spent several miserable nights like this and I was beginning to think that I was getting nowhere.

Steve and me with a reticulated python.

Rosie the boa constrictor has a fascination for our visitors.

Then quite unexpectedly, after a couple of weeks of Rosie ignoring me, she tentatively stretched out to my side of the sofa. It wasn't a huge breakthrough—just a few tongue flicks and she was back to her side of the couch—but it was a first step. After a few more weeks it was impossible to eat dinner because she was all over me. Rosie's favorite move was to slither up to the top of my head for a look around, her body firmly constricted around my face for support! By the time we filmed "Sleeping With Crocodiles," Rosie was sitting on the table while I did my bookwork or hanging from my shoulders while I did my housework.

During the filming I had to turn on the heat lamps for our wild boa constrictors. This was something that I would never have been brave enough to do if I hadn't got to know Rosie first.

I can't say that I would ever trust our wild snakes, but Rosie is so tame that sometimes even visitors get to meet her.

Some of the wildlife that comes to stay with us seems to prefer civilization to living in the bush. Take, for example, the female brushtail possum that found her way to us after she'd been hit by a car. When she arrived, the good folks who had found her sitting alongside the road weren't sure if she'd live at all. She really was quite a sight. Most of the fur had been scraped off one side and her left eye was hanging out on her cheek.

As horrible as she looked, after a quick visit to the vet and a relatively simple operation to remove her eye, she was on the road to recovery. After a couple of weeks she was well enough to be released and Steve built a cage for her high up in a tree out in the scrub behind the zoo. Every day for a week I would climb the ladder and give her fresh food and water. On the eighth day I was confident that she knew this was her new home and so I opened the door of the cage.

Although I continued to put food at the cage for another week, I never saw her. I was a little sad that she was gone, but knew she would be happily living in the wonderful eucalyptus trees. Over the next few months I thought of her often, especially when I put treats out for the other possums that lived near our house.

Steve holding one of Australia's special native species, an echidna.

As a rehabilitation zoo, Steve and I are often called on to care for sick and injured animals.

Apparently the word had spread that it was much easier to live at Steve and Terri's house than in the bush. Then, almost two years to the day after releasing my little brushtail possum, I noticed a brushtail with an obvious joey in her pouch, happily munching on some bread in our backyard. Upon closer inspection my heart soared. The mother possum had only one eye.

Sometimes I have had to be cruel to be kind. Such was the case with Jack the jabiru. I don't usually name the wild animals that come and go through our zoo, but Jack was different. Jack would not be leaving. He came to us from Fleay's Fauna Centre on the Gold Coast where he'd been cared for over several weeks while he recovered from a collision with a power line. Sadly, Jack had lost a wing in the accident and had gone through two operations to repair the area where the wing had been torn off.

The jabiru, or black-necked stork, is a magnificent bird. When I first met Jack I was impressed with the fact that he stood nearly as tall as me. I could see fear in his beautiful black eyes and he chomped a warning with his enormous bill. I could also see that he'd scratched up his lovely long, orange legs and learned that he had cuts on his feet, too. Because Jack couldn't fly, he would be on his feet more than a normal jabiru, and it was imperative that his feet did not become infected. Such infection can lead to a condition called "bumble foot" which is extremely difficult to treat and is sometimes fatal. Jack, of course, didn't understand all of that and had no idea that I was trying to help him.

Twice a day I'd catch him (avoiding that long beak) and place his feet in a bucket of warm salty water. We would sit together for twenty minutes and then I would put a special ointment on his cuts and scrapes and let him go. This went on for several weeks until he was well. Jack now lives in the wetlands section of our zoo with a brolga, several species of duck, two magpie geese, and some beautiful black swans. Although Jack has been King of the Wetlands for years now, he has never forgotten me or what I had to do for him. Our zoo staff can enter his area and Jack will approach them out of curiosity or for food. But not me. To this day, when Jack sees me he runs!

Amelia the wedge tailed eagle.

Steve feeding an alligator during a demonstration at the zoo.

By far the most rewarding part about living and working at our zoo is the education factor. The only way wildlife conservation is going to work is if we all learn how to live with nature instead of being afraid of it or wanting to dominate it. Whether it's koalas or crocodiles, we must begin to understand that animals have rules just like people do. If we play by the rules we can coexist quite easily, even with the most awesome predators.

During our numerous demonstrations every day here at the zoo, we show visitors how certain animals function in the wild. Whether it's an otter catching her own fish, or a saltwater crocodile trying to catch the keeper, every demonstration is a learning experience.

There is one demonstration that is slightly more dramatic than the others. Every year in Australia, some three hundred people are accidentally bitten by snakes. These people weren't trying to catch or kill the snake in question, they were simply minding their own business when contact was made. Usually this happens by someone accidentally stepping on a snake or reaching underneath something where a snake is dwelling. Most of these bites are from harmless non-venomous snakes, but we teach people to treat any snakebite as venomous. We bring out large pythons (all pythons are non-venomous) for visitors to view and even pet at the end of the demo, as well as show exactly how a pressure bandage works, and what will happen at a hospital.

I had been doing snake demos for more than a year, continuing to study snakebites and learn more about first aid, when the unexpected happened.

It was about 4:30 P.M. and the zoo had been closed for half an hour. Jan, our mammal keeper, and I were finishing up in the souvenir shop at the entrance. I heard a vehicle pull up, but I didn't think much of it as people are always coming in after hours with injured wildlife. As I approached the front gate to see what kind of animal needed our assistance, I saw a woman helping a teenage boy out of her car, the teenager appearing to have twisted his ankle. He was leaning heavily on the woman as he limped toward the entrance.

"He's been bitten by a snake," the woman replied. As she helped the boy to sit down on the ground, she further explained that she owned and operated a banana plantation up the road. The teenager was employed to pick bananas for her and he'd accidentally stepped on a brown-colored snake about ten minutes earlier. I looked down at the boy's leg. Just above his ankle were two incredible fang marks. This was a

Brown snake.

textbook bite. I could already see dark bruising around each fang mark and there was a slight trickle of blood owing to the venom's anticoagulant property.

I told the lad to remain calm, but I think it was more for my benefit than his. He was doing everything right, sitting down, not getting excited. I, on the other hand, knew that this was a serious bite and had to think clearly and quickly. I went to the first aid kit to grab a pressure bandage. We always made sure that three were rolled up, right on top. But as I looked in the box, to my horror, I saw that the pressure bandages were gone. Instead, there were only packets of white gauze in plastic wrappers. I didn't know it, but the staff had just changed the brand of pressure bandage. Jan and I hadn't been told and so we didn't recognize the new kind. Instead, Jan and I grabbed some towels so we could start working on containing the venom in the boy's leg. "Get Steve," I said quietly to Jan through clenched teeth.

All this time I was watching the clock. The towels were bulky, but I wanted to get pressure all the way up the boy's leg before too much more time elapsed. In less than two minutes a puffed Steve arrived with the necessary pressure bandages. He put them on, nice and tight, right over the towels. After pinning a note to the bandage, which indicated the time of the bite as well as the time the bandage was applied, Steve carried the boy to the car. As Steve got the boy comfortable in the back seat, he instructed the woman to drive straight to Nambour Hospital. Meanwhile, Steve called the hospital so they'd be ready.

It wasn't until the next day that we got a call to let us know that the boy had been discharged and would be fine. He'd received the proper anti-venom after the doctor had swabbed the bite site and discovered that the bite was from a common brown snake—the second most venomous snake in the world.

Steve and I are very lucky to live and work with what we love best. Zoo life definitely has its ups and downs but there is nothing else we'd rather be doing. It's our goal and our passion to open everyone's heart to love and care for wildlife for generations to come.

Chapter IX

"Old Faithful"

Crocodiles live in beautiful family units similar to ours. A happy, healthy crocodile family has a big adult male croc "dad" who is very dominant and commands respect, one to several adult female "mums," and their children. Usually when their kids are babies, they are protected, guarded, and nurtured. Youngsters are tolerated and teenagers are pushed out into the world to find their own territory. Crikey, I love crocs, and the more I understand their complex family structure the easier they are to love.

From the 1940s to the 1970s the two Australian species of crocodiles, saltwater and freshwater crocs (salties and freshies), were hunted for their skins and products. This intensive hunting pressure was responsible for a significant decline in crocodile densities throughout Northern Australia. In Northern Queensland, salties were driven to a critical level and the majority of accessible crocodile habitat was frequented by professional crocodile hunters, amateur shooters, and poachers. Surviving adult crocodiles in these areas became people-shy, or succumbed to the hunter's bullet—shot dead or maimed.

Terri and me with a freshwater croc.

In 1974 both species were declared totally protected fauna. This protection of Queensland's crocodiles has resulted in some recovery of both species. However, salties are currently categorized as "vulnerable," just one step from endangered. Certainly the populated East Coast of Queensland contains very low densities of crocs. In 1985 the Queensland National Parks and Wildlife (now the Department of Environment) established the East Coast Crocodile Management Program. This program was designed to alleviate "problem," rogue, or nuisance crocodiles conflicting with people. Any crocodiles reported to the Department of Environment (DoE) by tourists, residents, or professionals are examined individually by DoE rangers. Animals deemed dangerous or a potential threat are evaluated and then monitored or captured and relocated to Australia Zoo or back to the wild where they won't have a conflict with humans again.

Unfortunately, there are several problems I've recognized with the current capture/relocation of large adult male salties. Removing dominant males from their territory allows smaller, less dominant males to move into these territories, upsetting the crocodiles' social structure, which adversely affects the entire ecosystem. Releasing large males back into the wild places pressure on and creates conflict within existing crocodile populations, particularly in remote areas with existing dominant males.

After many years of understanding the problems attached with removing large dominant crocodiles from their domains, I decided to try an innovative technique to deter a designated problem crocodile in Lakefield National Park from approaching people, with an emphasis on minimizing impact on the ecosystem or the crocodile structure. Now was the time to accept the beauty of the crocodiles' family structure and try something new. I had to stop an inquisitive "daddy" crocodile from scaring people, without upsetting his immediate family and the entire balance of nature.

Lakefield National Park

The Queensland State Government in November 1979 gazetted Lakefield National Park with a total of 1,326,000 acres. The park is situated on the eastern side of Cape York Peninsula and comprises a major portion of the Laura Basin, extending for one hundred miles along its longest axis northward from the peninsula township of Laura.

Lakefield's climate is tropical and monsoonal. Rainfall is thus strongly seasonal, with ninety-five percent of the average annual rainfall of 430 inches falling between November and April—the "Wet Season." Significant rainfall events rarely occur during the rest of the year, which is the long, dry season.

The major portion of Lakefield is undulating or lowland plain country, and it is drained by an extensive river system, which empties into Princess Charlotte Bay. During the annual wet season the various rivers and tributaries flood and many interconnect and spill over, covering vast areas of floodplain. Up here in Far North Queensland, when it rains—mate, does it rain! It buckets down, causing flash floods in minutes.

With the progression of the dry season, water levels gradually regress and stream flows slow down and eventually stop. However, very significant numbers of permanent waterholes and shallow wetlands remain. These we call billabongs.

In addition to the various freshwater habitats and the associated saline estuary systems, the park contains a wide diversity of vegetation communities. These include a variety of tropical woodlands, heath, and open forest, gallery rainforests and semi-deciduous vine thickets. A large belt of grassland lies across the northern section of the Park, inland and adjacent to extensive plains. Vast wetlands, which comprise both marine plains and mangrove forests, fringe the tidal river systems and adjoin virtually the entire coastline. Lakefield is the most pristine crocodile habitat. It's gorgeous.

Crocodiles on Lakefield

The seasonal and permanent billabongs within Lakefield National Park, and the vegetation and animal communities they support, form a natural wonder of very significant conservation value. In particular, Lakefield affords protection for the largest population of both salties and freshies

A juvenile freshwater crocodile. Look how ferocious I am!

on Queenland's East Coast. The national park is one of only five key areas for saltwater crocodile conservation in Queensland, and furthermore, it contains the largest populations of this species within any protected area in the state.

Park rangers have monitored crocodile numbers, local distributions, and activities through formal surveys, incidental observations, and reports from park visitors.

Lakefield has long been a popular, remote area for self-reliant travelers, and up to fifteen thousand people annually camp at the 132 campsites scattered throughout the park. Visitors come to explore and appreciate the park's natural and cultural values, with recreational fishing also being a major attraction. The majority of visitors desire to see a "crocodile in the wild." The fact that almost all the park's camping areas are sited beside permanent billabongs containing populations of at least one species of crocodile readily affords such sightings and other potential interactions with these majestic reptiles.

"Old Faithful"

During 1994, an increasing number of reports were received by park rangers of a large salty displaying what was regarded as nuisance behavior at "Old Faithful Waterhole," a popular fishing and camping area on the Normanby River.

The crocodile concerned, estimated to be at least fourteen feet in length, was regularly swimming close to, and approaching, people in fishing boats and campsites located on the high riverbank. The actual truth of his so-called nuisance behavior is that the poor old croc was just inquisitive of the people in his territory—he never, ever had a go at anyone or demonstrated any aggressive behavior toward people. I guess when a huge crocodile head, looking like a dinosaur, pops up near your camp or boat, it's quite intimidating. Actually, it was scaring the living daylights out of visitors. What a shame! I do not understand why park visitors were complaining about him, but looking at people crashing around in your territory is hardly nuisance behavior.

After a series of complaints, the park rangers surveyed the waterhole and immediately spotlighted the crocodile. In an attempt to deter him from continuing his nuisance behavior, two rounds of .308 were fired over his head. This technique appeared to have the desired effect for several months, and then visitor complaints started to increase again.

Following assessment by park rangers, the area was closed to visitors to reduce potential risks to both park visitors and the crocodile. The rangers were concerned he might be injured or killed by illegal shooting. It was then I was asked to try my alternative management strategy. Given the problems associated with capture/relocation of large, dominant male crocodiles, it was decided to capture, hold, and harass the animal for a short period of time prior to release in the same waterhole, with the intentions of instilling a reasonable fear of people, i.e., "people shyness." If successful, this method would ensure the continuation of the crocodile social structure and overall ecological health of this section of the Normanby River, and reduce the potential risk of negative interactions between this crocodile and the future visitors to the national park.

So I planned an action aimed at trapping and educating "Old Faithful," the name given to the dominant male crocodile of this section of the Normanby River. It's very Australian to give things you love nicknames, and I reckon "Old Faithful" was a top name for him.

Trapping "Old Faithful"

As soon as we arrived at Old Faithful Waterhole, we noticed a large crocodile watching us 160 feet away, in the middle of the billabong. As we prepared a dinghy to survey the area, the crocodile, inquisitive of our presence, was watching us while slowly moving upstream; only his head was visible. He was magnificent! Big gnarly head. What a beauty!

After launching my black croc dinghy, we idled toward the deepest section of his billabong. After rounding a bend, a large crocodile was observed watching us from 260 feet away,

Terri and me checking "old faithful" trap two.

midstream. Only his head was visible, yet it was high out of the water. As we slowed to a stop, the crocodile acknowledged our presence by exposing his nuchal scutes (those big dinosaur-like plates on his neck), followed by his entire back, for approximately twenty seconds, then he submerged his back, leaving only his neck and head exposed. He swam casually into the shade of a large overhanging melaleuca tree where he once again displayed his entire back, neck, and head for approximately twenty seconds. This obvious display of size was considered a threat posture, directed at us. Awesome! He was threatening us and posturing to let us know we were in *his* territory, and this is how big I am. "Yep, you're big all right," I shouted to him. Starting the outboard, we headed in his direction. He allowed us to get within two hundred feet before he eventually submerged. This deep, shady section of his billabong was considered an ideal location for a trap site.

I examined the billabong's only exposed mud bank, and instantly located fresh slides of an animal estimated at fourteen to fifteen feet as well as fresh slides and wallow of an animal estimated at eight to ten feet. It was concluded that these crocodile signs belonged to the so-called nuisance male crocodile and his female mate. They utilized the mud bank for basking and ambushing feral pigs and other prey. The combination of the crocodile activity and the accessibility made this area another ideal trap site.

After many, many hours of hard yakka over two days, I, Terri, and my team from Australia Zoo, headed by my best mate Wes Mannion, and a couple of DoE Rangers headed by my good mate Barry Lyons, erected two traps at the sites. Dad and I designed our trapping techniques in the early 1980s. It's a very simple design, which ensures absolute minimum stress or injury on the crocodile, utilizing soft mesh and breakable strings. This is our design (Fig. 1):

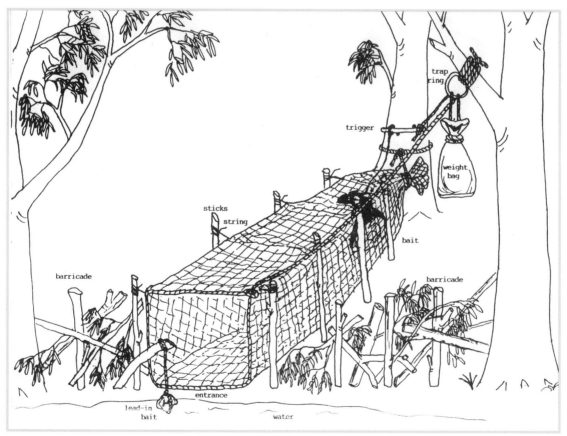

Figure 1

The traps were anchored to large trees with a half-inch rope and baited with a ninety-pound portion of fresh meat, which was secured by a short quarter-inch rope with a spliced loop over the trigger mechanism. Any jerking or pulling of the bait would release the trigger mechanism, causing the weight bags to fall and pulling the mouth of the trap closed in a drawstring effect.

Logs, branches, and foliage were erected as barricades around the trap to eliminate the possibility of a crocodile approaching the bait from the sides. Hence, the only access to the bait is via the trap entrance, and the crocodile has to enter the trap to reach the bait. Lastly, lead-in baits were attached by a three-millimeter rope directly in front of the trap, dangling over the water. This represented a token feed of pork to initiate a feeding response at the trap entrance, where the bait inside the trap was visible to the crocodile.

The whole time we were setting up the traps, Old Faithful and at least one of his girls were watching us from about 160 feet away. They were obviously very bold, inquisitive, and quite possibly hungry.

The first night after the traps were set I couldn't sleep, for I could feel the uncanny sensation of knowing a croc had already gone into trap one. We arrived at the trap site at six o'clock the next morning to find my instincts verified—caught in the trap was a stocky 8.5 foot

"Old Faithful," the best looking crocodile I'd ever seen.

female. She had entered the trap at around nine the night before. She was *gorgeous*! And very grumpy. So I quickly opened up the trap entrance and let her out. She was free and back in her billabong in a couple of minutes. Although she hissed and bared her teeth in retaliation, she was quite calm and ladylike. Not once did she try to kill me, which is rare for a trapped croc—normally they go ballistic, biting everything and anything.

The next night was the same again, I couldn't sleep. I could virtually feel the big old male croc staring into the trap from the safety of his billabong, the tantalizing odor of pork luring him closer and closer. At 11:55 P.M. the rush of plummeting weight bags and the trap being triggered pierced the stillness of the night. All night I could hear the commotion of a crocodile in the trap, although we never heard any loud head thrashing, which suggested that the trapped crocodile wasn't fighting for his life, but rather that he was confused and endeavoring to push his way free. I know to never approach a trapped crocodile until daylight. The danger and stress of approaching him at night would have deadly repercussions.

At first light I revealed that our target crocodile had been trapped. A strapping big bloke! By 6 A.M. I had two jaw ropes in place and the exhausted crocodile was secured.

Interestingly, the mouth of the trap had drawn closed around the base of his tail and cloaca, a common occurrence in previous captures of crocodiles over twelve feet. To ensure no cloacal damage, Old Faithful was easily persuaded all the way into the trap. Once he was restrained inside the trap with the two top-jaw ropes, a canvas shelter was erected and he was kept damp and monitored closely. His head was almost two feet long and his total length was fourteen feet. He had no signs of nose rub or abrasions and was considered to be in prime condition, with substantial fat deposits around the neck and the base of the tail. His teeth were massive and in good condition. He possessed no obvious scar tissue from territorial disputes with other males. He was a "steamer," the best looking crocodile I'd ever seen. An absolutely huge, muscular, powerful crocodile for his size. He exploded with the fury of being trapped—hissing and gnashing his massive pearly teeth. Despite his numerous bursts of aggression and struggle, while I tried to secure top-jaw ropes, Old Faithful never made any attempts to bite me, even when I was working close to his head. I am amazed and in awe of this pristine modern day dinosaur's reluctance to kill me. I still can't believe that not once did he strike directly at me. Never had a killer streak in his entire body. We love you, Old Faithful, you're a big beautiful bloke.

Now comes the most intricate and important process of all. Every instinct with crocs I've gained had to be harnessed to educate this magnificent fourteen-foot apex predator, king of the billabong. It's now that I have to teach him, for the safety of his entire family and home. My educational process was based on achieving three main objectives: instilling "people shyness" (stopping the crocodile from approaching people, and ensuring the crocodile cannot be approached close enough to be shot); maintaining the crocodile's social structure and ecosystem; and reopening the waterhole to visitors.

Wes and me struggling with an adult saltwater crocodile.

During the afternoon of the day he was captured, Terri and I circled the water immediately in front of the crocodile in two different sized dinghies, demonstrating to the crocodile the noise and nature of the vessels and the people driving them. He responded by becoming agitated when an outboard motor was started. He became even more agitated when he heard an approaching or starting 4WD vehicle. His obvious aggravation was considered a positive sign that he was learning to fear boats and vehicles. Our campsite was in his full view, and in addition to this Terri and I camped with Old Faithful, allowing him to see, hear, smell, and sense the vibration of people in close proximity. He acknowledged our presence by watching us closely and tensing his body when we approached him.

During the night I further harassed Old Faithful in a dinghy with spotlights. Mimicking an illegal crocodile shooter, I stalked as close to him as an illegal hunter would shoot, then fired several .444 rounds into the water and the mud bank within two feet of him. It breaks my heart to subject the king of this territory to such extremes, but if he doesn't learn he will most certainly be killed. If I can't teach him to stop approaching park visitors, Old Faithful, his family, and the entire ecosystem will be destroyed. I have no qualms putting my life on the line to protect crocodiles. I will die defending them. It causes me great pain and anxiety to inflict fear on this poor old croc, but without me, he and his wilderness would suffer. At six o'clock the next morning he was calm and motionless. However, when the first outboard was started he reacted by becoming distressed and fighting to break free. A similar desperate attempt to escape occurred when a vehicle approached the camp. These were considered positive signs of stress activated by human activity. My education process was obviously working extremely well.

Old Faithful's final lesson was "the power of people." At six-thirty, eight people straddled and restrained the big crocodile for fifteen minutes, while the trap and top-jaw ropes were removed. Under the weight and power of the people, he hardly attempted to fight; this was considered the perfect response to a feeling of being overpowered.

On the count of three, everybody jumped off the crocodile and he was free. Without hesitation he slowly walked into the shallow water and swam to the middle of the billabong with

People power holding down "Old Faithful" prior to his release.

his head above water; then he headed straight toward the deepest section. Later that day from a totally camouflaged position, I watched him swimming and basking in the deep, shady section of his billabong.

He appeared to be alert, behaving normally and reunited with his mates. One of his gorgeous girls was right alongside him, obviously happy to be with him. Overall, I was satisfied Old Faithful had responded well to our entire trapping/educational procedure and felt confident that he would remain the dominant male crocodile within his territory, thus ensuring the continuation of their pristine ecosystem. Mission accomplished.

In February, after the wet season, Old Faithful Waterhole was reopened to the general public. The three campsites were occupied by campers, who reported no nuisance crocodile behavior to the rangers.

Then in July we surveyed the waterhole to determine the extent of the crocodiles' "people shyness." During this period Old Faithful was not observed day or night, despite our finding his fresh tracks, slides, claw marks, and basking areas. On several occasions a crocodile with a total length less than ten feet, as well as two juvenile salties (Old Faithful's children) and approximately twenty freshies of various sizes, were observed.

During this survey we discussed crocodile activity with fishermen camped on the waterhole. We were told how three fishermen in their late forties saw the "fifteen-foot Big Old Crocodile" waiting for them at the boat ramp. We examined the bank where they moored their dinghy, finding a slide matching a crocodile less than ten feet, which had been feeding on offal, backbones, and carcasses left on the bank by the fishermen.

Misinterpretation of crocodile behavior and exaggeration of total and head lengths are common traits for park visitors and tourists. These practices, combined with careless activities around waterholes and providing unnatural food sources for crocodiles, make it difficult for park rangers to determine bona fide nuisance behavior and an appropriate management strategy.

Again in October we surveyed Old Faithful Waterhole. Upon arrival, we observed Old Faithful and a female (approximately 8.5 feet in length) sunning on the opposite bank. The animals appeared to sense the approach of our vehicle and quickly slid into the water and submerged. Old Faithful was then observed swimming upstream toward the deep hole. This activity was considered to show intimidation by the presence of people. During this survey period, we very briefly observed Old Faithful surfacing to breathe, look around, then submerge (usually under the camouflage of overhanging vegetation).

Our sightings were brief, lasting less than forty-five seconds if he could not observe us, and less than ten seconds if he could observe us. All sightings were in the vicinity of his deep hole, which indicated that this was his refuge. We also observed that he had three females, which we estimated to be between eight and ten feet, beautiful looking sheilas. I'll bet he's a great lover and proud father.

The congregation of his happy family in this deep hole prompted us to measure the depth of the entire Old Faithful Waterhole. Excluding the shallows—those areas with less than forty-inch depths—the average depth was thirteen to fifteen feet. Only one small hole, at twenty-seven feet deep but less than thirty-three feet wide, was measured. This one small, deep hole was their only refuge and was also favored by large barramundi. Because this hole was being utilized for refuge by the crocodile family during people visitation, and was a preferred fishing spot, sightings of large crocodiles by park visitors were inevitable.

Now that Old Faithful has been educated to avoid people, the *greatest* task of all time is being tackled—education of the people who visit crocodile territory. To keep both crocodiles and visitors safe, all people visiting wilderness areas should be well educated and totally respectful of the crocodiles' family structure and their territory. It's the toughest job of all! Terri and I will continue to film our interaction with crocodilians to maximize the education of potential visitors to our national parks and the conservation of the special reptile. Crocs always have and always should rule! We just need to understand their rules.

Chapter X

Bindi

Steve came in late one night. This wasn't unusual; he often got caught up in a project. Sometimes he would be building a huge rock formation for a new enclosure here at Australia Zoo, or maybe he'd be digging a new crocodile pond with his trusty old backhoe. But tonight was different. There was no clanging of tools or hum of machinery. The zoo was quiet and still; only a stream of smoke from Steve's fire gave away his location. Was he planning a new filming adventure? I couldn't imagine what was going through his mind, but I sensed that he needed some time on his own. His dinner got cold and I put it away. I was doing some paperwork when I heard the door close quietly and Steve walked in.

"What's going to happen to the zoo?" he asked.

I couldn't figure out what Steve was talking about. Everything was running well with the zoo and nothing was about to happen.

"When we're gone, what's going to happen to the zoo?" This time Steve sounded almost panicked. He had been sitting by that fire for hours reviewing his life, growing up with all these animals. Some would outlive us by many years. His concerns were quite valid. We were up most of the night talking about our hopes and dreams for conservation and Australia Zoo. There was no doubt in our minds about the next step to take. Steve and I both grew up with a burning passion for saving wildlife. Now we needed to pass on this desire to make a difference in the world. We'd made the big decision. More than anything on Earth, we knew that we wanted a child.

Steve's enthusiasm and joy at the prospect of having a baby was extremely contagious. It became a topic of conversation at Australia Zoo, during film shoots, and at every family gathering. Everyone was happy and excited at the thought of a little Irwin running around, but we had some practical points to work out, too. After all, our lives were hardly normal. Filming wildlife documentaries all over the world and living in the middle of a zoo surrounded by wild animals would make having a child even more challenging. We were determined to set some ground rules right from the start. We both felt strongly that we stick together as a family and encourage our little one to follow dreams wherever they led, even if that meant something other than wildlife conservation.

It was after a whirlwind trip to America, filled with awards, banquets, and promotional events, that I came home to discover that I was pregnant. I was amazed to see Steve at loss for words when I told him.

"Congratulations . . . I love you," he stammered as he gave me a big hug and a kiss. He was then on the phone for hours telling everyone the good news. I didn't realize he knew so many people.

We had reveled in our happy news for only a few days when we received an urgent phone call from far North Queensland. It was the peak of the dry season and some of the crocodiles were in serious trouble. Many younger crocs were having great difficulty traveling the distance from their drying water holes to more permanent bodies of water. One enormous old fresh-water crocodile refused to leave a farmer's canal. He had dug himself into the tiny bit of water remaining, but it was fast disappearing. There was no time to waste. We contacted the film crew and headed for the tropics.

I was lucky to have a doctor with common sense give me advice for my pregnancy. He told me that I didn't need to change my lifestyle since I'd become pregnant, but that I shouldn't take on any new or different physical challenges. I was in good health and got the OK to continue filming. The main caution Dr. Voucollo and Dr. Tarr gave me was regarding the heat. It was more important to avoid getting overheated, particularly during the first trimester.

As we drove north I began to realize what a challenge this was going to be. The summer heat and humidity was heavy like a wet wool blanket. We had to drive into a very remote location and then pack up for a hike across country to the farm. An epic journey!

We arrived just before dark after driving two days nonstop. It was too late to survey the plight of the crocodile, so we made camp. I was amazed at how tired I was. Every little task was an effort and I was asleep before I hit the swag.

At first light I woke up to Steve boiling the billy. Still tired from the long trip, I had a quick cuppa before gearing up for the big hike ahead. Steve had to think of everything we might need to help this crocodile. We packed ropes, tarps, blindfolds, knives, food, and a lot of water. Steve carried most of the equipment, including some of the camera gear, and we headed out. By mid-morning we all began to feel the effects of the sun blazing relentlessly down on us. I knew that I was slowing the group down as I stopped to cool down in every available shade. Nobody complained about our slow progress. I continued to push on, keen to reach the crocodile that so desperately needed our help.

It was after noon when we finally reached a small series of canals. Most of them had dried out completely, but one, deeper than the other, still held a bit of moisture—and one cranky crocodile!

We all felt a sense of urgency as Steve scrambled to get the ropes and tarps ready for the move. I felt my adrenaline kicking in as Steve was preparing to jump this eight-foot freshie. The rest seemed like a slow-motion blur. I remember Steve on the croc's head and shoulders as I jumped its back end, restraining the crocodile's powerful tail. The mud was much deeper and softer than I'd expected. It was incredibly slippery, and difficult to hold the struggling croc. Steve was shouting for me to pick him up, but I couldn't move. The suction of the mud had a firm hold on my legs and I felt strangely weak, unable to stand. I felt Steve shift his grip to take more of the crocodile's weight, then suddenly drop the croc's head back in the mud. It was only after the immense struggle to the top of the canal that I discovered why Steve hesitated so abruptly. While he was trying to drag me and the crocodile out of the mud, the frightened freshie picked his moment and snapped down on Steve's hand. In an instant, Steve's hand was crushed. One of croc's teeth had broken off in Steve's thumb, leaving Steve severely incapacitated.

Even though the crocodile did make it safely to a new billabong, and Steve's hand eventually healed up just fine, I realized that the next few months would be very different for us. I would have to be much more careful about backing up Steve while I was in this "delicate state."

As the months passed, the weather began to cool off a bit and my body began to adjust to the demands of pregnancy. We were planning a documentary shoot in the Galapagos Islands. I knew this would be my last chance to film overseas before the baby was born and I was incredibly keen to go. Given my history of working in the heat, Steve was concerned about carting my huge tummy directly to the equator, but the giant Galapagos land tortoises compelled me to go. After all, our tortoise Harriet was collected from the Galapagos Islands in 1835. More than anything I wanted to see where she came from.

I was in my last trimester as I waddled onboard the catamaran that we would call home for the next few weeks. The crew welcomed us onboard and a couple of them even spoke a little English—bonus! Below deck we visited our quarters. Steve and I shared a room that was quite nice and

Another adventure—me in my delicate state with a gopher snake.

unbelievably small. There was one tiny window above the bed and a little fan that rattled terribly. And then there was the heat. Even though we were out on the ocean, there was absolutely no sign of a breeze. The air was still and it was hot—easily the hottest place I had ever been.

That night the crew prepared us a lovely dinner and we enjoyed the magic of the wildlife all around us. We decided to turn in and get an early start the next morning. Little did we know, the sleeping arrangements themselves would be an adventure! The small bunk was situated close to the ceiling and the little room was like an oven. Since Steve's a very light sleeper and would be up a lot during the night, I chose to sleep next to the wall. We both lay there, drenched in sweat with no breeze and a very loud fan puffing a bit of air over us. I finally heard Steve's breathing change as he fell asleep. I tried to relax enough to go to sleep myself, but it was difficult in a room that eerily reminded me of a crypt. The more I thought about the cramped quarters, the less inclined I was to rest. As an added drama, I then felt the call of nature. I wasn't sure how I'd do it, but I felt compelled to try and slither out of my bunk and sneak to the rest room without waking Steve. Inch by inch I slid over Steve, who was in a deep sleep. Just as I was about to clear the other side of the bunk, the slope of the ceiling caught me. There I was with my big tummy wedging me firmly between Steve and the ceiling. Steve woke with a start—he must have thought one of the local sea lions had him!

Although the nights were long, the days were filled with fantastic wildlife. Nothing was afraid of us and we were able to swim with the seals, sea lions, marine iguanas, and even penguins! The land animals were just as spectacular. We watched the lava lizards fighting for a mate, the land iguanas eating the local vegetation, and even my favorite: the precious giant tortoises. After hiking all over the volcanic islands all day, John Stainton (our director/producer) worked hard to make sure there were ice packs available on the boat to keep my tummy cool. Just like the animals around me, I learned to survive the heat. Some of the animals didn't seem to take any notice of the weather. The flamingos always looked busy as they marched around the pond, sifting through the water for food, and the blue-footed boobies were hilarious as they courted each other by showing off their beautiful blue feet, first holding one foot up high, and then the other. It may have been more difficult to get around while I was so pregnant but it was definitely worth the effort. I have special memories of the Galapagos Islands that I will treasure for the rest of my life.

Back home in Australia we were busy putting the final touches on a shark documentary that we'd been working on for nearly two years. Steve had gotten to know several species very well. We would routinely go hang out with one particular group of tiger sharks who seemed to have gotten to know us, too! Even the giant fourteen-foot-plus females would swim lazily around our dinghy as if to get to know us better. Steve spent many hours in the shark cage having a wonderful time with these deep-sea giants. I was having fun observing from the boat, but the fifteen-hour days in the middle of the ocean were starting to take their toll. At more than eight months pregnant, my body just couldn't put up with the constant movement out on the water. My doctor told me that it was time to hang out closer to home. Steve would have to tackle the bull sharks on his own.

Steve was worried about leaving me on my own for long periods of time even though the baby wasn't due for another two weeks. He decided to film the bull sharks on the local river systems so that he wouldn't risk being stuck in the middle of the ocean if anything happened. The night before he was to head south to search for bull sharks, I thought my water broke . . . but I wasn't sure. It was nothing like I'd heard or read about, and not wanting to worry Steve, I just quietly made an appointment to see the doctor the next day.

In the morning it was business as usual at Australia Zoo. Steve had driven only two and a half hours away when he found a good filming location and I merrily drove off to the hospital around lunchtime for a checkup. After a brief examination, Dr. Tarr gave me the news: I'd better call Steve because I was about to have a baby.

Steve was always so calm—even in the face of death—but I could hear the panic in his voice over the mobile phone. I told him not to rush, but I could hear him yelling for the crew to hurry as he hung up. Why was he telling the film crew to hurry? Sure enough, by mid-afternoon, in came Steve, the cameraman, soundman, and John Stainton. I knew some dads bring a video camera, but this was ridiculous!

Since my water had broken the night before, there was some concern that the baby needed to be born soon. Therefore, my labor was induced. It really was an amazing process. Under Dr. Tarr's instruction, the midwife just dialed my contractions closer together. As the machine released the drug through the IV into my arm, the pain became more intense. Finally, at about 6 P.M., they announced that I'd be going into the delivery room. That's when I asked for some kind of pain relief, only to be told that I was too far along for anything but nitrous oxide—a kind of "happy gas." That sounded great to me until I tried it. One breath and I felt terribly nauseous. The only option I had left was to dig my fingernails into Steve's arms and legs. I'm still not sure why that made me feel better!

Steve proved to be an inspirational coach. No matter how tired I got, he would convince me to push even harder. I felt a bit like a prizefighter, as he'd give me a play-by-play description of what I needed to do next. As the baby's head began to emerge, Dr. Tarr called for Steve to help. Grasping the baby's head gently but firmly, Steve started to pull. The baby's shoulder hung up for a minute and then it was all over.

"It's a girl," came Dr. Tarr's voice through a haze. We were both surprised. This would mean my parents finally had a granddaughter, since both my sisters had boys. Steve and I had never discussed girls' names much, but as he held our brand-new baby, he sounded certain when he said he wanted to name her Bindi. It was the word aborigines use for young girl. It was also the name of one of Steve's favorite crocodiles.

"Bindi Sue," I said, thinking of Steve's little dog Sui.

Steve immediately took off to show the entire maternity ward his beautiful Bindi Sue. Never mind that they all had their own new babies, Steve's enthusiasm could not be

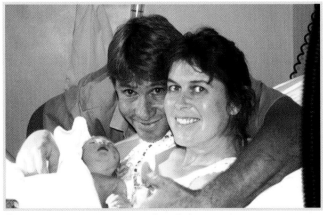
Steve and me minutes after Bindi's birth.

stifled. After about an hour, the midwife was beginning to worry. "Is he coming back?" she queried. Just then Steve returned with a very content little Bindi. She had just gone on her first adventure with her dad—and there were many more to come!

Bindi was born on a Friday night, July 24, 1998. We had a wonderful weekend together watching the rainbow lorikeets and honeyeaters on the bottle brush trees outside the hospital window. I told Bindi all about the exciting life that awaited her and we both caught up on some much needed sleep. The first of the week was upon us in no time and with it came the unescapable commitments of Australia Zoo. Steve's dream for the zoo included expanding our property before surrounding housing developments squeezed us into one small area. This was the day we were to close on another thirty-five acres adjoining us. Bindi was restless, as if she knew something important was going on. We bundled her up and headed for home, but stopped at the attorney's office on the way. Not even three days old, Bindi's first trip into the big wide world was to take another step toward securing her future with wildlife conservation.

We hadn't been home long when the advice started pouring in. It seemed everyone had an opinion on how to raise the newest Irwin. Some said not to take her outside for at least six weeks, others said not to let her ride in the car, and I even heard criticism for wanting to take Bindi to the office with me. Luckily, Steve and I had already planned that no matter what, we'd be together as a family. I felt in my heart that if we just showered Bindi with love, we couldn't go wrong. So it just made sense that Bindi should go with us on a day shoot with sea turtles. Bindi was now six days old. We rode with John Stainton because there just wasn't enough room in Steve's car. I've never seen John drive so carefully. Bindi didn't mind a bit. She slept most of the day and hung out with the soundman when it was my turn on camera. The day went so smoothly, we knew that we'd made the right decision. Bindi wouldn't just be a part of our lives at Australia Zoo, she was ready to hit the road filming wildlife documentaries, too.

Bindi was just two weeks old when we took off for her first international film shoot in the United States. The trip had been planned for some time and we thought Steve would be going on his own. What a wonderful turn of events that Bindi came early enough that we

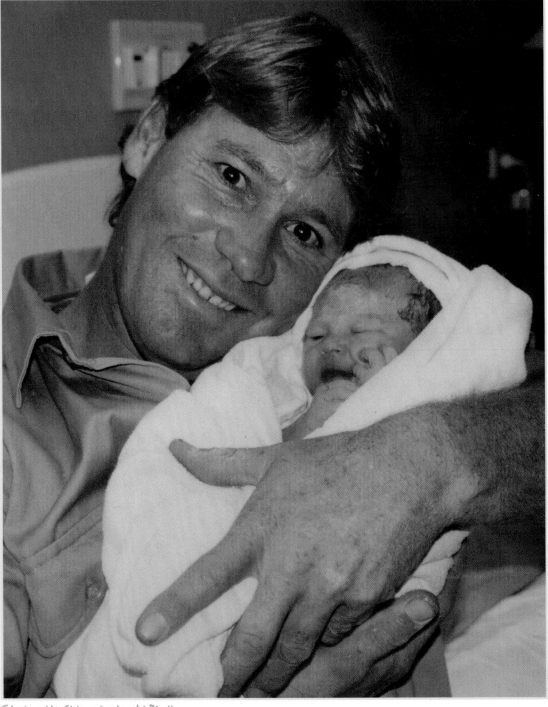

Steve with five-minute-old Bindi.

could go, too. Bindi took the long flight in her stride, sleeping most of the way from Brisbane to Sydney to Los Angeles. The flight attendants commented on how tiny she was, as she could lie down on an airline pillow with room left over! Our first stop was California, where among other things we filmed the California brown tarantula. Bindi seemed intrigued by the giant spiders, trying hard to focus on them when they would stroll past. She didn't mind the huge arachnids one bit, but coming from Australia's winter to Southern California's summer made her more than a little cranky. When she got hot and mad, her whole body would go red. It did make things a bit easier for me: when Bindi got air-conditioning, I got air-conditioning!

Our next stop was Texas, where we hired a small aircraft to get us into a tiny little strip in the middle of a remote national park. We arrived just before dark in torrential rain. We were thirty miles from the nearest accommodation and the rental car was nowhere to be seen. Luckily there was a pay phone at the airstrip so we could call the rental vehicle people. We were shocked to find out that, with the rising water due to the rain, the woman with the rental car was afraid to pick us up. We tried to explain our situation: the pilot had to get the plane out before dark, we had a baby with us, and we were basically stranded. Much to our amazement, she still wouldn't come. Just as we were about to start searching for some kind of shelter, a pickup truck came bouncing down the track. Inside was a very kind Mexican-American schoolteacher, and his pet Chihuahua. Bindi was quite content to snuggle down into her car seat and there was just room enough for both of us, and a bit of critical camera gear, in the front of the pickup. Steve and the crew all hopped in the bed of the pickup and prepared for a long, wet, uncomfortable ride. In spite of one or two tricky creek crossings, we made it safe and sound. Bindi looked very peaceful as she slept right through. Our first day in Texas and the adventures had already begun!

In the morning the sun was shining as if there never was a storm the night before. We started out early in search of the ruins of some local homesteads. We were hoping to check out likely areas for snakes well before the heat of the day. Any snake species would do, but Steve was really hoping to find some big beautiful rattlers.

As we approached the first dwelling, we could see that it had been built to last. The timber roof had rotted away, but that was understandable considering the house was well over a hundred years old. The rock walls were made well and truly still intact. They had only started to crumble away and still provided shade and shelter for any wildlife living inside.

Steve went in first and immediately began turning over every bit of timber and rubble on the floor.

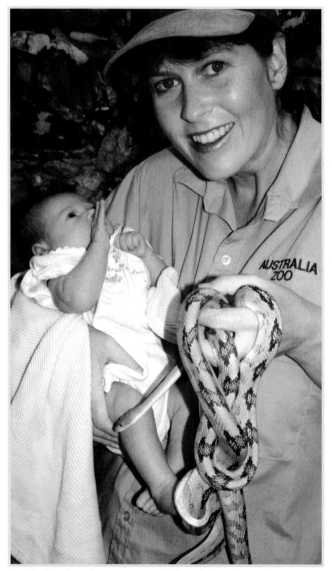

Bindi's first snake experience. Love at first sight!

Suddenly I heard the all too familiar call, "Snake!" as Steve spotted movement in the corner of the room. As I rushed over with Bindi, I could see not one, but two snakes moving away from us. As Steve gingerly picked one up, he noticed that not only were these snakes nonvenomous, they seemed uninclined to bite. While Steve was showing me their beautiful coloration and lovely nature, one stretched out toward me as if to investigate what I was all about. Since I was holding Bindi, I could only put out one hand for the snake to rest on. The next thing I knew, Bindi raised her tiny fists in the direction of the snake and stared intently at it, trying to hold focus. Both snakes were now coming over to check out this little person. As they flicked their tongues in and out, smelling Bindi in an attempt to identify what she was, Bindi continued to show interest. This was Bindi's first snake experience and already we could see that the die was cast. She absolutely loved snakes. Definitely a chip off the old block!

Our first overseas film shoot with Bindi had been a real success. She turned out to be a wonderful traveler and seemed as happy on the road as she was at home. We arrived back at Australia Zoo in time for her one-month birthday. Steve was getting more confident when he held Bindi and really wanted to give her a tour of the zoo. After

Bindi and me.

all, someday this could all belong to her. Each day Steve would introduce Bindi to a new animal and she loved it! By the time she was two months old, Bindi had met every animal at Australia Zoo. She touched a boa constrictor, went in with the alligators, and attended numerous crocodile demonstrations.

Bindi's education with wildlife had begun. With some of the most dangerous animals in the world literally in her backyard, Bindi would have to learn a lot more than caution

Bindi loves riding the motorbike with her dad.

with hot stoves and busy roads. In much the same way aborigines have raised their children for the last forty thousand years, we would have to teach Bindi how to coexist with the natural world. After all, wild animals would become part of her daily encounters.

Steve loved spending time with Bindi and would take her with him while he was working on new enclosures. She became so keen on visiting the zoo sites with him that the sound of the motorbike would cause her to react. Bindi loved to go putting around the zoo with Dad on the bike.

By the time Bindi was a year old she had already become such a seasoned traveler with half a dozen trips to America and numerous trips filming around Australia, I didn't think anything would faze her. A film shoot in Florida would prove me wrong.

Steve and I had received a request from Elgin Air Force Base to relocate a problem alligator. The eight-foot-plus gator had become too accustomed to receiving handouts from humans and had lost its fear of people. It would only be a matter of time until the alligator became large enough to pose a real threat, and it was decided to move it to a more remote area on the base. This made for an excellent filming opportunity and a lucky break for the alligator. Most "pest" alligators end up in a farm where they are killed to make boots, bags, and belts. Our air force gator had a chance for a much happier ending.

Bindi's favorite animals are snakes. She loves them! (Photo courtesy of Queensland Newspapers Pty Ltd)

We arrived at the water hole to find the most fearless alligator that we had ever encountered. Steve had a fish on a string and the alligator walked right out of the water and straight up to Steve. This was one fearless, dangerous alligator. Once Steve got a rope over the alligator's head, it was simply a matter of jumping on the alligator and holding him down until he could be moved to his new home. Even though we had help from several of the Jackson Guard, this alligator was not going to give up easily. He simply started walking back to the water with five of us lying on him! This wily gator seemed to take great pride in dragging us through some nice deep, sticky, smelly mud. We were all covered from head to toe before we got that overgrown lizard stopped! Once we finally got successfully moved into the back of a waiting pickup truck, it was a quick trip to his new (and remote) pond. After the alligator was released we were all very happy and excited . . . except for Bindi. She had waited patiently long enough and began to wail for some tucker. Since she was still breastfeeding, I knew this would settle her right down. So I headed for a private spot to spend some time with her. Bindi took one look at me and started crying even louder. She seemed a bit panicked, like she didn't know who I was.

Bindi waxes Daddy's surfboard.

Then I realized my mistake. I was so covered with mud that I was unrecognizable. The mud had soaked right through my clothes and I smelled like a swamp. Now what was I going to do? Once again, it was Steve to the rescue. He waded right through a nearby pond and couldn't find any alligators in it. He then handed me some soap, towel, and an extra set of his clothes from his backpack. I took a quick tub—really quick in case there was an alligator in that pond that he missed—and Bindi and I were back in business!

It's an unfortunate reality that Bindi can't go filming everywhere in the world with Steve. Some areas are too much of a disease risk for Bindi (malaria, yellow fever, and more) and some areas just have too much political unrest. When we decided to film a documentary right across Australia it meant that we could all be together the whole time. Bindi wasn't quite old enough to walk when we bundled her into the DC-10 and headed west.

After takeoff, Bindi was delighted to discover that she was allowed out of her seat to crawl and climb all over the plane. There was heaps of room, and since we flew under ten thousand feet, the view was spectacular. Australia's interior is a brilliant mosaic of red and brown desert. Some of it is made up of incredible rock formations and occasionally we would even find some water. The highlight of my trip was landing at Ayers Rock. The mighty rock, known as Uluru by the aborigines, has been a sacred site to the indigenous people for tens of thousands of years.

As we approached this magnificent landmark, we all felt that this was a place of immense spiritual significance. The local aborigines did not believe in climbing the giant rock, and we respected their wishes.

Bindi sat at the base of Uluru with us, happily munching away on all the red sand she could shove into her mouth, when she suddenly started trying to stand and crawl up the huge rock. Steve and I weren't sure what she was doing, but we tried to help by supporting her so she

Bindi with Harriet.

wouldn't slip over. Bindi placed her hands on the rock and gently rested her cheek against it. She closed her eyes and stood that way for some time. Steve and I looked at each other. We both had goose bumps. Bindi had made us both feel a bit eerie and unsettled, as it appeared she was "listening" to the rock. Finally she crawled off after a little lizard and the spell was broken. This was to be the first of many unusual bonds that Bindi would make with nature. Her intuition is incredible. She will often worry about an animal before Steve and I discover that it's sick or injured. This uncanny connection reminds me of the abilities Steve has with wildlife, a strange sixth sense that we refer to as "the force."

This bizarre instinct with wildlife seems to be an Irwin trait that has been handed down from Bob and Lyn to their son Steve, and now Bindi.

We always treasured the time we would spend with Steve's parents. Bob was the wrangler, showing Bindi every snake and lizard that passed by. Bindi learned early on that some snakes were "hot" (our word for venomous) and couldn't be touched. She proudly pointed out a large, highly venomous western brown snake on a camping trip when she was just two and a half years old. Bob would let Bindi wrangle the occasional harmless small carpet python and Bindi demonstrated the Irwin family finesse with each and every one. From snakes to koalas, Bindi's "Poppy" enthused her to love the natural world.

It was Steve's mother, Lyn, who instilled in Bindi a compassionate heart for all wildlife. Bindi's "Gran" showed her how to approach everything from kangaroos to echidnas. Like all children, Bindi can be a bit rough at times, but through Lyn's patient guidance, Bindi learned to always be gentle and quiet with animals. I see Lyn in Bindi's mannerisms and I see Lyn in Bindi's eyes. Bindi was only eighteen months old when she lost her Gran, but she lives on in Bindi's soul. If you ask Bindi where Gran is, she will smile and say, "Gran is an eagle." Every time I see an eagle fly over, I am reminded that Bindi's Gran is still watching over her.

Although I cannot predict what the future will hold for Bindi, I am sure of one thing: Bindi will continue to be a protector of wildlife. She will fight to defend the animals she loves and she will have a special place in this world. With a father like Steve, who regularly lays his life on the line to defend the wildlife he loves, how could Bindi be any different? I will do my best to make this world a better place for Bindi, and I'm really not terribly worried about her. Life will be filled with adventure and challenge and I know that Bindi will do well. She has to. Like her family before her, Bindi is a wildlife warrior.

Bindi showing her dad the crocodiles.

Chapter XI

Saving the World from Beerwah

Times are changing for zoos around the world. No longer are zoos simply a venue for displaying nature's weird and wonderful wildlife. Today, zoos must evolve to take on much more responsibility with regard to regional and global conservation. I am proud to say that Australia Zoo continues to be leading the way with strategies that incorporate people as well as animals and their habitat. We firmly believe that if people are struggling for survival, wildlife issues are at the bottom of the list. But if we can make an effort to help ensure that everyone has healthy children with full tummies, we can more successfully achieve our conservation goals.

Steve and I also operate Australia Zoo with a philosophy that might not seem to make the best business sense. Since 1970, the Irwin family maintained a strict policy that the needs of our animals will always come first, our team will come second, and our visitors rank third. Although it sounds odd not to put the customer first, the reality is just the opposite. With incredibly healthy and happy animals, our team has higher morale and overwhelming passion for their work. Patrons of Australia Zoo win, too, because they experience our enthusiastic team and zoo animals as they've never seen them before.

With our "Wandering Wildlife" program, we are taking many animals out of their enclosures to interact with people. You could encounter almost anything, like a koala, a box tortoise, a shingleback lizard, a cockatoo, a peregrine falcon, dingoes, giant pythons, and much more. With some animals, like the kangaroos and wallabies, you enter their area with them. Still other animals, like our otters, Tasmanian devils, and crocodiles, may not be ideal for visitor interaction, but they sure love to have a go at a keeper! Not only is all this activity excellent for our animals' psychological health, it instills in everyone a greater desire to look after these animals in the wild. That's the bottom line. That's what it's all about. That's why Steve and I work so hard at Australia Zoo, filming wildlife documentaries, shooting movies, promoting our wildlife toys, and even writing this book.

We are inviting everyone to join our team and work together to protect our wild world. The single greatest contribution an individual can make to save wildlife is to simply not purchase *any* wildlife product. The illegal wildlife trade is a multi-billion-dollar market, surpassed only by the illegal drug trade. Some wildlife products are obvious. Most of us would never dream of buying a

monkey paw ashtray or an elephant leg umbrella stand. But most products are far subtler: turtle shell combs, snakeskin hatbands, emu oil, or alligator skin boots. The consumer doesn't need any of these things. They are simply novelty items and trinkets. Until we

Helping an adult male red kangaroo with a broken leg.

stop the legal trade of wildlife products, we don't have a hope of enforcing laws against the illegal trade.

Australia Zoo incorporates a three-step approach to wildlife care: protecting habitats, preserving species, and rehabilitating individual animals. We firmly believe that losing sight of any of these areas would be detrimental to conservation. When it comes to preserving species, so many are in the "endangered" category it can be a bit overwhelming.

With valuable input from our zoo director, Wes Mannion, we have developed a state-of-the-art Endangered Species Unit (ESU). This facility is designed to mimic the needs of endangered species in the wild. No expense has been spared making sure these off-display animals are content enough to breed successfully. For some, it's the first time they have reproduced in captivity anywhere in the world. The knowledge we are gaining will not only help us to secure animals in captivity, but also replenish wild populations.

We are very proud to have accomplished this with the canopy goannas of Far North Queensland. After our world-first breeding, the offspring were released (along with the parents) in the exact territory—the very tree, in fact—from which they came. And with several babies hatched, and seventy more eggs in the incubator, we're about to do the same thing with the critically endangered rusty monitor. With the important data that we have collected and published, we can

Another endangered species, the rusty monitor.

be confident that these species have a promising future. Our current challenge is the Fijian crested iguana. Love is in the air, and with any luck, we will soon hear the pitter-patter of ever more scaly little feet. And lest you think the ESU is only a haven for our reptile friends, we're working with cassowaries, wombats, koalas, bilbies, frogs, and otters . . . just to name a few!

Steve isn't just discovering new ways to help animals in captivity; he's discovering new animals in the wild, too. One of Steve's most famous finds happened way back in the early eighties. He was surveying a river of crocodiles with his dad when he saw an unusual flash of white in the water. With Steve's usual enthusiasm, and total disregard for unspotted crocodiles, he jumped straight in the river to check it out. Although it managed to elude him, Steve identified this creature, with its white head and pink nose, as a strange turtle, the likes of which he'd never seen before. Steve couldn't have been more right. Some years after his first encounter, he brought one of these strange turtles in for identification. Not only was Steve's discovery exciting for the world of herpetology, he also had the honor of having a newfound species of turtle named after him: Irwin's Turtle, *Elseya Irwini*.

Irwin's Turtle, *Elseya Irwini*, a tortoise named after Steve and his dad.

When it comes to conservation, Steve and I aren't just focused on the big picture. We are devoted to the needs of individual animals, too. Every day we receive dozens of calls asking for help with some kind of critter. Sometimes it's with concern for an animal that may have been hurt, and sometimes it's with concern that an animal may have hurt someone. So whether it's a koala that's been hit by a car or a brown snake in somebody's bedroom, we're off in a flash to give aid.

We have two rescue vehicles designed to respond to any animal emergency. From emus to crocodiles, we can wrangle absolutely anything. We provide twenty-four-hour care for any wildlife requiring rehabilitation whether the animal is sick, injured, or orphaned. We've constructed a complete "Vet Block" to provide any necessary veterinary care. This is a huge annual expense for Australia Zoo, yet a conservation component that we cannot ignore.

Thankfully, most of our wildlife rehabilitation efforts have a happy ending and the animals can be set free. But in many cases, the recovered wildlife shouldn't go back to the location in which it was found. The busy road, pack of dogs, or illegal shooter are still there . . . the very thing that caused the problem in the first place. So Steve and I picked some suitable habitat (2,000 acres of it) in the outback. Managed by Steve's dad, Bob, this facility has become a haven for a myriad of spectacular wildlife. It's our very own Garden of Eden, where wildlife is safe from the dangers of civilization.

Will Steve and I ultimately succeed in making a positive difference for the planet? With your help, we're sure to win. Now more than ever we are all becoming more aware about the need to conserve our precious living heritage. What will I leave behind for Bindi? I will leave her the truth. We are surrounded by lying wildlife perpetrators, hiding behind the cloak of "science." The day will come when sustainable use, controlled culls, scientific whaling, and other lies will be exposed and become atrocities of the past. The truth is that we will never save wildlife by killing it. Together, we can work to protect the inhabitants of planet Earth. If we save our wild places, we will ultimately save ourselves.

Terri and I are totally dedicated to conservation. Our passion for wildlife is our elixir of life and we'll die defending animals that others deem dangerous and threatening. Our work is to challenge those who continue to carry on with medieval attitudes such as "the only good croc is a dead one," "the only good shark is a dead shark," "there's a snake—quick, kill it." Terri and I work to make those old, ugly, anti-wildlife attitudes extinct.

We humans still have a long way to go with learning to live harmoniously with our environment and its wildlife. For example, as you're reading this paragraph, our whales and dolphins are still dying painful lingering deaths.

I've seen dolphins and whales enjoying human interaction. I've heard stories of them

Swimming with the dolphins—you've gotta love 'em.

saving people from drowning. We reward them with death, disease, and destruction. Our oceans and waterways continue to be dumping grounds for toxic waste bacteria and other pollutants, slowly but surely killing our magnificent cetaceans. Dolphin-friendly tuna makes me laugh—Terri and I have stopped eating tuna until the tuna nets cease killing tens of thousands of dolphins every single year. There are still countries that kill dolphins for use as crab bait!

Two years ago I was diving at Cape York Peninsula when I noticed some movement twenty feet below me. It looked like a shark in distress and I quickly powered down. As I got closer and closer I became horrified, nearly vomiting into my snorkel. On the sandy bottom of the ocean were the bodies of several live sharks with all their fins amputated. They couldn't swim or move. I was so disgusted and distraught I wanted to cry. Shark fin fishermen had caught the sharks and, while they were still alive, cut off all their fins and then tossed them overboard to die a painfully slow hideous death. Reality check: Think about having your arms and legs cut off, then being left in the sun to die slowly.

It never ceases to amaze me how cruel some people are. Do you think people would be so merciless and torturous if fish and sharks cried like babies when they felt pain?

I'm disappointed when I consider the fate of our crocodilians. Out of the twenty-two-odd species, most are classified as vulnerable or endangered, the threat of extinction ever-present. I find it fascinating that the world's crocodilians survived the great dinosaur extinctions and have been on this planet for nearly 200 million years, in excess of 180 million years before humans ever started to evolve. They are the true survivors—modern-day dinosaurs.

Terri with an endangered Fijian crested iguana.

After existing for nearly 200 million years, crocodiles have been nearly exterminated in sixty years by hunters with high-powered rifles. If we can't learn to *live* with such predators, our future is dismal. Imagine Africa without lions, Australia without crocs, the oceans without sharks or dolphins and whales. Who'd want to live here? Not me! So Terri and I push hard— real hard. Every single day of our lives involves wildlife education. We must teach, spread the word, the wildlife gospel. Crocodiles and sharks are only dangerous to those who make the mistake of breaking the ecosystem's rules.

The greatest contributing factor to croc attack in Northern Australia is alcohol and, guess what? Crocs don't drink.

With excessive alcohol consumption come bravado and stupidity. Next thing you know the "It'll never happen to me" attitude takes over and people try to share water with crocodiles. Now, crocs don't run out onto the highway and rip you out of your vehicle by the jugular. They don't drop out of trees and tear your arms off, either. And kids, they definitely don't live under your bed. No, you've got to enter into their domain to get into a conflict with these huge reptiles.

Statistically there's only one crocodile-related human fatality per year in the whole of Australia. There's more danger on the road traveling to Northern Australia than there is camping by a river with a healthy crocodile population. Thank God crocs aren't evil, malicious creatures that do like to eat people because we're amazed at the hundreds of people every year who make the mistake of swimming where they know there are crocs. Terri and I couldn't resist filming a family of tourists in a river where we were trapping rogue crocs. They casually wandered down to the water, draped their towels over the "WARNING—CROCODILES INHABIT THIS RIVER" sign, and happily swam and frolicked with their children in the water. Crazy stuff!

Luckily our wildlife park and our wildlife documentaries are the perfect vehicles for the educational approach to conservation that Terri and I push. The latter have been seen by millions of people around the world. But while preaching the message of global wildlife conservation,

Waterholding frogs. Like canaries used by miners of old to give them warning of poisonous gases, these tiny amphibians act as environmental indicators.

we're careful to acknowledge that our own Australian backyard is in need of cleaning up. Australia has one of the worst mammalian extinction rates in the world. We're currently destroying vast areas of rainforest, mangrove, wetland, and desert, all in the name of progress. And as we continue to receive scientific verification of the ways in which we are killing the world's wildlife, each of us needs to take time to consider every single way we are contributing to the detriment of the environment.

I plead with every single businessperson who reads this book to focus on rectifying any damage your business processes are doing to the environment. The time has come when all of us must be held accountable. We don't own the planet Earth, we belong to it. And we must share it with our wildlife.

The single greatest threat is loss of habitat. We can breed endangered species in captivity but with nowhere wild to release them their days are probably numbered.

Now is the time to preserve and protect what habitat is remaining.

It's obvious that every man, woman, and child can contribute to the well-being of our native wildlife and the planet through simple day-to-day stuff such as recycling, chemical and pollution awareness, and not wasting water.

As for Terri and myself, our aim is to continue producing more wildlife programs to entertain and enlighten. We'll take the audience to some of the wildest and remotest territories in the world. I gain more power and understanding of animals if I'm right in among them, and I'm finding myself doing more and more of the filming, as it's hard or too dangerous to get a cameraman in as close as I want to be. Hearing, smelling, and seeing the animal and its surroundings is always my prime objective.

Almost fifty percent of my time is spent on filming; the other half is taken up with our zoo, which is our base, and from here we're saving the world—from Beerwah.

Isn't she just gorgeous?

Epilogue

Our Wildlife Force

It was the greatest day of my life. My mum and dad drove me into the small gravel parking lot and I jumped out of the car and beckoned impatiently as Mum and Dad locked it up. They knew how excited I was—reptiles, especially snakes, were my passion and I had longed to get a firsthand glimpse at these amazing creatures in living color. I couldn't wait for my parents and stormed in.

As I entered the zoo, my eyes suddenly fixed on a large glass panel; a slight movement caught my eye, and as I drew closer, a wave of golden brown flashed before my eyes. *Fierce snake!* I screamed with delight. It was the snake I had dreamed about seeing my whole young life. The world's most venomous snake! My eyes were as big as dinner plates, and just as I thought I would explode with excitement, a sweet voice came from behind me.

"Can I help you?"

I spun around and it was Lyn Irwin, Steve's mum. She had a big smile and was gently coaxing a small eastern grey kangaroo to lap from a dish of milk. Beneath her,

The Glasshouse Mountains where we live.

three more joeys looked up lovingly, with only their heads protruding from their artificial pouches.

She gave them a motherly glance, and content with that, the little orphans tucked their heads back into the warmth of their pouches. My eyes were now fixed on Lyn as she tended to some tourists, taking money and packaging some souvenirs without the little joey even missing a sip of milk. By that time, my mum and dad had caught up and Lyn returned their change. Lyn gave me another big motherly smile and directed us toward the exhibits. I danced down the path brimming with excitement for what lay ahead in this wonderful place. I raced past a group of kookaburras laughing in the early morning sun and took a quick glimpse at a curlew, which would later become one of my best mates.

A little further down the path, I came to another glass panel, and before my eyes lay the most spectacular animal I had ever seen. It was a reticulated python some twenty feet long and weighing over three hundred pounds. She looked into my eyes and her beauty was mesmerizing. Slowly she flicked out her tongue and the light glistened in a rainbow of blues and pinks on her skin. Her scales shimmered in a kaleidoscope of color. We had looked into each other's eyes for what seemed an eternity when I heard voices behind me.

"Take her, Stevo." I swung around. "Hang on to her, mate!"

I could just see a flash of commotion through the trees. I bolted toward the melee and pressed my face hard up against the fence for a closer look.

"I've got her head!"

"Keep the weight on, she's building up!"

A flash of black scales and human skin whirled in a sea of water. Violently, a big old gator twisted and turned, and the two men atop her hung on tenaciously.

"Hang on, Stevo, she's going again!" yelled Bob Irwin in a commanding voice. Bob and Steve worked together as one, and slowly, Alison the alligator tired and began to give in. Quickly, Angus, the zoo's vet, moved in and closely examined Alison's jaw, quickly suturing a large gash on the top of her mouth that she'd sustained in an altercation with Daisy, her normally gentle mate.

"Clear!" Angus yelled when his job was done.

"One, two, three," Bob called in a steady voice and both he and Steve were off and clear of the alligator before I could blink. A huge smile erupted on Steve's face and he let out a hoot of excitement. Bob, not one for a lot of emotion, gave a wry grin and said well done. The two scaled the fence with ease.

"How about some smoko?"

"Sounds great." All three headed off for the traditional morning tea.

My jaw dropped to the ground. I couldn't believe what I had seen. I spent the rest of the day following Steve and Bob's every move, and from that moment on, I realized my calling. I had stumbled into a magical place, a place where wildlife reigned supreme. Where creatures who are persecuted and hated because of human ignorance and misunderstanding are loved and nurtured. Where visitors are excited and at the same time educated about these beautiful creatures. A place where everything else pales in comparison to the well-being and protection of wildlife. It had evolved from a family of extraordinary and dedicated people, and I had walked into the heart, soul, and beginning of Australia Zoo.

Fifteen years have passed since that day, and the core values created by Bob, Lyn, Steve, and his two sisters Joy and Mandy have not changed. Back then, Australia Zoo was called the Queensland Reptile and Fauna Park, and since those amazing early days, our Australia Zoo family has grown to over one hundred members. The size and shape of Australia Zoo has changed with the times, and today it encompasses over thirty acres, with over 150 acres planned for future development. We have one of the finest zoological facilities in the world, and our success with breeding some of the world's most endangered species is a testimony to this.

Our mission statement—"Conservation through exciting education"—is the driving force behind our family. We hold this deeply in our hearts. If you can't excite people about wildlife,

In the early years, here I am after catching a sand goanna.

how can you convince them to love, cherish, and protect our wildlife and the environment they live in?

Australia Zoo is riding on a wave of passion and enthusiasm. We are here for the conservation of wildlife right across the globe. This deep-seated passion has come from the beginnings of Australia Zoo's history, and has created a wildlife "force" which has reached millions of people in every corner of the earth by virtue of Steve Irwin, television's Crocodile Hunter, his entire family, and the staff of Australia Zoo. The message is simple: love and conserve our wildlife.

The Australia Zoo team celebrating after a successful crocodile relocation.